Shelagh Bourne
500 Duplex Avenue.
Apartment 2107.
4830841.

Glendon '74 - '75.

THE RUSSIAN REVOLUTION

and

LENINISM OR MARXISM?

The Russian Revolution

and

Leninism or Marxism?

by Rosa Luxemburg

New Introduction by Bertram D. Wolfe

Ann Arbor Paperbacks for the Study of Communism and Marxism
The University of Michigan Press

Fifth printing 1972
First edition as an Ann Arbor Paperback 1961
Introduction copyright © by The University of Michigan 1961
All rights reserved
ISBN 0-472-06057-0 (paperbound)
ISBN 0-472-09057-7 (clothbound)
Published in the United States of America by
The University of Michigan Press and
in Don Mills, Canada, by Longman Canada Limited
Manufactured in the United States of America
Leninism or Marxism? was originally published in
the United States as *Revolutionary Socialist Organization.*

CONTENTS

By Bertram D. Wolfe

ROSA Luxemburg and V. I. Lenin were born in the same year, 1870, and their lives were destined to touch and cross at many points. Though they were both called "revolutionary" socialists, their diverse temperaments and their differing attitudes on the nature of socialist leadership, on party organization, and on the initiative and self-activity of the working class, kept them poles apart. Indeed, the two short works which make up the present volume are sharply critical appraisals of Lenin's penchant for personal dictatorship over his party, the dictatorship of his Central Committee over its locals, and the dictatorship of his party and its leaders over the working class and society as a whole. These critiques from Rosa Luxemburg's pen are among the most important works to have come out of the Socialist or Second International, for, without ever using the word or the concept, totalitarianism, Rosa Luxemburg had a prescient feeling for the totalitarian potential in Lenin's views. Today, as we look at the party and the state which Lenin founded, we can no longer doubt that in this controversy Rosa Luxemburg was prophetically right.

1

PORTRAIT OF ROSA LUXEMBURG

Most of the political life of Lenin and Luxemburg was lived out in the old pre-war Second International, founded in 1899, which collapsed in the holocaust of war in 1914. That vanished world of international socialism possessed no more original, ardent, dynamic, and attractive figure than that of Rosa Luxemburg.

She was born in an "enlightened" Jewish merchant's family in the small town of Zamosc, in Russian Poland, near the Russian border. To say then that a Jewish family was "enlightened" was to suggest that it had broken out of the circle of ghetto culture and traditions and absorbed the general culture of the country. Rosa's parents were at home in Polish, Russian, and German literature and thought. This cosmopolitan background made the young girl take easily to internationalism. Lenin, too, used the term "internationalist" frequently. But, whereas she was to be active and a leader in the affairs of three parties, the Polish, the Russian, and the German, and in the International Congresses and Bureau, Lenin, wherever he lived, remained a Russian in exile, with gaze fixed on Russian affairs and Russian party squabbles.

Physically, the girl Rosa did not seem made to be a tragic heroine or a leader of men. A childhood hip ailment had left her body twisted, frail, and slight. She walked with an ungainly limp. But when she spoke, what people saw were her large, expressive eyes (beautiful eyes judging by her photographs), glowing with compassion, sparkling with laughter, burning with combativeness, flashing with irony and scorn. When she took the floor at congresses or meetings, her slight frame seemed to grow taller and more commanding. Her voice was warm and vibrant (a good singing voice, too), her wit deadly, her arguments wide ranging and addressed, as a rule, more to the intelligence than to the feelings of her auditors.

She had been a precocious child, gifted with many talents. All her life, to the day of her murder in January 1919, she was tempted and tormented by longings to diminish her absorption in politics in order to develop to the full the many other capacities of her spirit. Unlike so many political figures, her inner life, as expressed in her letters, her activities, her enthusiasms, reveals a rounded human being. She drew and painted, read great literature in Russian, Polish, German, and French, wrote poetry in the first three of these, continued to be seduced by an interest in anthropology, history, botany, geology, and others of the arts and sciences into which the modern specialized intellect is fragmented. "Interest" is but a cold word for the ardor with which she pursued her studies. A passage from one of her letters written from prison to a young friend, Dr. Hans Diefenbacker, in the spring of 1917 will suffice to give an inkling of this passion:

> How glad I am that three years ago I suddenly threw myself into botanizing, as I do into all things, with all my ardor, with the whole of me, so that for me the world, the party, and the work vanished, and one single passion filled me day and night: to tramp about out there in the fields of spring, to fill my arms full of plants, then, back at home, to systematize them, put them in order, identify them, enter them in notebooks. How I lived in a fever all that spring, how I suffered when I sat before some little plant and could not ascertain what it was and where it belonged! . . . In return

for that now I am at home in the green world, I have conquered it for myself—in storm and passion—and whatever one seizes upon thus with ardor has firm roots in one.

It would not be amiss to suggest that this longing "to conquer in storm and passion" was what made Rosa Luxemburg a "revolutionary" rather than a "reformist" socialist.

Having been brought up in Russian Poland at a time when its intellectuals were "discovering Marx," her initiation into the revolutionary movement was precocious, too. At sixteen, when she graduated at the top of her class from the girl's Gymnasium in Warsaw, she was denied the gold medal because of "an oppositional attitude towards the authorities." Three years later, at the tender age of nineteen, she had to flee to Switzerland to avoid arrest, aided both by a Catholic priest, who was given to understand that she was escaping from her parents to undergo conversion, and by an underground Polish movement.[1]

At Zurich she made simultaneous entrance into the world of refugee politics and the university. At the latter she won two doctorates, one in law the other in philosophy, acquiring at the same time her life-long interest in a half dozen other disciplines. She got to know Plekhanov, Axelrod, Lenin, and other Russian exiles, and three Polish exiles who worked with her thenceforward, Marchlewski, Warszawski, and Jogiches.

Leo Jogiches, three years older than Rosa, was already a fully formed conspirator and revolution-

---

1 It was the only time she fled arrest. Thereafter, she was to take prison terms as part of her work.

ary when he fled to Zurich in 1890. Almost immediately they became linked by a lifelong personal intimacy (without benefit of religious or civil ceremony) and by a lifelong association in the Polish and Russian, and later in the German, movements. The two were as different as two people engaged in a shared life and common enterprise could be. Jogiches was taciturn, stern, gloomy, secretive about his past and his private life, with none of her eloquence or outgoing capacity for friendship. Moreover, he was, as she was not, a consummate conspirator, an able organizer, a natural-born faction fighter. Under the conditions of underground life in Poland and Russia it is doubtful if she could have built a movement without him. She was the ideologist, he the organizer and conspirator. In Germany, however, where life was lived more publicly, he became a leader only by following in her wake.

Switzerland was too small and peaceful, the political life of a Russian-Polish exile too confined, to give scope to her large talents and aspirations. She went for a while to France, where it is a measure of the breadth of her personal criteria that she was able to form friendships both with the outstanding Marxist leader, Vaillant, and with the great leader of the socialist "right," Jean Jaurès. "A splendid human being," she said of the latter, "open, natural, overflowing with inner warmth and intelligence." Her glowing temperament was closer to that of the humane, warmhearted Jaurès than to the more dogmatic Vaillant, the pedantic Kautsky, or the narrow, dictatorial Lenin.

The French movement was also too small to hold her, and she headed for Germany, the land where the "party of Marx and Engels" was the largest political party in the country and the largest and most influential in the international socialist movement. As a foreigner, she would find it impossible to become publicly active in Germany, so she proposed "marriage" to Gustav Luebeck, son of an old German socialist family she knew. After the wedding ceremony, the "couple" separated at the door of the marriage bureau, and "Frau Rosa Luebeck," a name she never used except to legitimatize her political activity, was free to plunge into the doctrinal and tactical disputes, the mass activities, the addressing of meetings and congresses, the writing for theoretical and popular journals. But not for that did she abandon her Polish and Russian activities, for this frail woman had enough overflowing spirits for three parties.

Almost at the outset she rose to the top of the great German party. She became a contributor to the theoretical organ, *Neue Zeit,* then assistant to its founder and editor, Karl Kautsky. She added her touch of fire to his doctrinaire fight against the "revision" of "orthodox" Marxism. She contributed to and became an editor of provincial dailies, then of the daily central organ, *Vorwaerts.* She got into the Vorstand (Executive), where even the veteran Bebel treated with respect her ardor, learning, wit, and sharp tongue. She became the teacher of Marxian economics at the Central Party Training School. Unlike other German pundits, who did little more than repeat Marx's formulae in "new" works, she developed first an original, mildly heretical interpretation of the labor theory of value,[2] then ven-

---

2 In her lectures, published posthumously in 1924 as *Einfuehrung in die Nationaloekonomie.*

tured to cross swords with Marx himself in a critical appraisal and revision of the master's arid and weak second volume of *Das Kapital*.[3] Finally, from 1905 on, this redoubtable woman ("one of the last two remaining *men* in the German Social Democratic Party," she once said of herself to Bebel)[4] became a leader of an extreme Left Wing which considered even the veterans of Marxist "orthodoxy," Kautsky and Bebel, to be a mere "Center" to her "Left."

LENIN AND LUXEMBURG AS
"REVOLUTIONARY SOCIALISTS"

When Rosa Luxemburg was murdered by Prussian officers in January 1919 while being taken to prison, the Leninists laid claim to her martyrdom, her tradition, and her name. On the surface this seemed a plausible claim. For both Lenin and Luxemburg regarded themselves as "revolutionary socialists." What they meant by this was that they rejected root and branch the society in which they lived, denied that it could be reformed or made better in any meaningful fashion, insisted that it must be overthrown in a great upheaval and replaced by a totally new society. One of Rosa Luxem-

---

3 This was the subject of her *Die Akkumulation des Kapitals: Ein Beitrag zur oekonomischen Erklaerung des Imperialismus* (Berlin, 1913). In this writer's judgment, her schemata are as far from economic reality as those of Marx which she was criticizing, but, be that as it may, hers is a work of undeniable originality and intellectual force, which has had a great influence on subsequent Marxist writing from Lenin's *Imperialism* to the various works of Fritz Sternberg.

4 The "other man" was her friend and disciple, Klara Zetkin!

burg's notable pamphlets, *Reform or Revolution* (first published as two articles in the *Leipziger Volkzeitung* in 1898 and 1899) was an attempt to prove that modern industrial society, the most rapidly changing in history, could not be fundamentally altered or improved except by a social revolution and that such reforms as had been instituted were a by-product of the revolutionary movement rather than voluntary acts of society to remove abuses and redress grievances. Legislation, constitutions, codified rights were but the "vegetative stage of society"; its "creative stage" was only and exclusively social revolution.

Both Lenin and Luxemburg were doctrinaire "lefts," too, in their rejection of the activities of the organized workingmen aiming at improving their conditions of life *within* the framework of industrial (or as they preferred to say, "capitalist") society. Both denied the possibility of any long-term improvement. Both had a low opinion of trade unions and of parliamentary activity. Neither could ever understand why workingmen in general were not more attracted to the historic "mission" which Marxism had assigned them; why workers had no stomach for being reduced to "nought" the better to prepare themselves for becoming "all."[5] They never noticed nor understood that it was *against being reduced to nought* that the real workers' struggle was directed.

---

5 Cf. the lines of the socialist song, "The International": "Arise ye slaves, no more in thrall,/ The earth shall rise on new foundations,/We have been nought, we shall be all!" Marx first used this formula, borrowed from the Abbé Sieyès who had applied it to the "Third Estate," in *Zur Kritik der Hegelschen Rechtsphilosophie* (1844).

It was their common underestimation and misprision of the changes going on in industrial society, their common low opinion of reforms and of trade union and parliamentary activities, that linked Lenin and Luxemburg together as "left" or "revolutionary" socialists. But here the resemblance between these two dissimilar temperaments ceases.

ATTITUDE TOWARD WAR

Their two names have also been linked by their opposition to World War I. But Lenin thought that a European war would be "a useful trick for the revolution" and "doubted that Nikolasha and Franz Josef will give us that pleasure."[6] He welcomed war when it came, as "putting the bayonet on the order of the day," marking the longed-for transition from the era of walking with "thin and weak soles on the civilized sidewalks of provincial cities" to the era that required "thick, hob-nailed boots" to climb the mountains. One of the "huge advantages" of any war, he said, was that it "mercilessly revealed, exposed, and destroyed much that is rotten, outlived, moribund in human institutions."[7]

In contrast with his fierce exultation that bayonets were now the order of the day, war came to Rosa Luxemburg as a burden of grief and anguish. The failure of the International to prevent it, or even decently to oppose it, above all the war-drunkenness of the ordinary socialist workers, plunged her

---

6 Letter to Gorky during the Balkan Wars, out of which grew World War I, *V.I. Lenin i A.M. Gorkii* (Moscow, 1958), p. 91.

7 Lenin, *Collected Works* (4th Russian ed.; Moscow), vol. XXI, pp. 184 and 222.

into despair; for a time she seriously contemplated suicide. She sought to have the shattered International purify itself by merciless criticism of its errors, re-establish the broken ties of solidarity across the frontiers, sober the war-drunk masses, and unite them for a common struggle to bring about an early and a just peace.

"The slogan of peace," Lenin declared, "is stupid and wrong . . . It signifies philistine moaning . . ."

And again: "The slogan of peace is wrong—the slogan must be, turn the imperialist war into civil war."[8] Luxemburg above all wanted the war to stop. Lenin wanted the war prolonged until the old order was in ruins, then prolonged further by its conversion into a universal civil war. Rosa Luxemburg was most concerned with the sufferings of the masses in war; Lenin with mobilizing their hatred. She wrote sadly of their chauvinistic madness; Lenin closed his eyes to, even denied, their chauvinism, picturing them as "betrayed by their leaders." She wished the International to be won back to its old prewar position, restored and purified. He proposed that the International be split, and a Third or Communist International built on its ruins. When he used his control of Russia in 1918 to call a conference to found a new international, her movement sent a delegation instructed to oppose its formation. But at that moment, her murderers silenced her voice. She was an ardent fighter for her views but not by choice a splitter. Lenin's method had always been to fight for his views by splitting whatever he did not control.

---

8 Lenin, vol. XXXV, pp. 121 and 125.

"LENINISM OR MARXISM?"

The work here published under the above title is made up of two articles Rosa Luxemburg wrote, in 1904, against Lenin's organization views and organization plan. The title is not hers. She called her articles, more modestly and matter-of-factly, "Organizational Questions of the Russian Social Democracy." They were published simultaneously in Russian in *Iskra,* and in German in *Neue Zeit.* They have since been republished in many languages as a pamphlet, under varying titles. In English, the United Workers Party published such a pamphlet some time in the twenties; then a fresh translation was made from *Neue Zeit* in 1934 by Integer, who entitled the pamphlet, *Revolutionary Socialist Organization.* Yet another version was published in 1935 in Glasgow, Scotland, by the Anti-Parliamentary Communist Federation, which gave it the title, *Leninism or Marxism?* The present volume uses the Integer text as the best translation, but has adopted the Glasgow title as the most attractive and best known in English.

In two pamphlets, and a number of articles published between 1902 and 1904, Lenin had been hammering away at his new organization plan for a "party of a new type," that is, one differing fundamentally from all previous Marxian parties, whether those founded while Marx and Engels were alive, or since. Besides Rosa Luxemburg many other Marxists active in the Russian movement published their criticisms of his view, among them being Plekhanov, Axelrod, Martov, and Trotsky.

Reduced to its bare outlines, Lenin advanced the following propositions:

1. Left to its own devices and insights, the working class is incapable of developing any conception of the "historic mission" which Marx assigned to it. "The *spontaneous* development of the workers' movement leads precisely to its subordination to bourgeois ideology . . . the ideological enslavement of the workers to the bourgeoisie" (Lenin, vol. V, pp. 355–56. Italics here and throughout as in the original). What the workers' movement spontaneously concerns itself with is a "petty-bourgeois" matter, the price at which it sells the goods it possesses, namely its labor power. It wants but to get the best price and the best terms under the present "bourgeois" system. To do this it may fight the employers and even the state, but it will never develop the "socialist consciousness" necessary to its "historic mission."

2. Such "socialist consciousness"

> can only be brought to the workers from the outside . . . Alone, by their own forces, the working class is capable of developing a pure-and-simple trade union consciousness . . . But the teachings of socialism have grown out of the philosophical, historical, economic theories which were worked out by the educated representatives of the possessing classes . . . (vol. V, pp. 347–48).

3. For this the working class needs a party which is not made up of the working class but a party of guardians, a self-constituted vanguard *for* the working class; an élite party drawn from all classes, made up primarily of declassed revolutionary intellectuals, who have made revolution their profession. This party should lead and guide the working class, inject its doctrine into the workers, infiltrate the workingmen's organizations and struggles, and seek to

use them for its purposes. Only "bourgeois politicians," Lenin wrote, can believe that the task of a socialist is to serve the workers in *their* struggles. The task of the socialist politician is "not to assist the economic struggle of the proletariat, but to make the economic struggle assist the socialist movement and the victory of the revolutionary party" (vol. IV, p. 273).

4. This classless élite, since it does the thinking for the workingmen and seeks to inject its consciousness into them, can appear even in countries where the working class is backward and weak. It is an élite which is drawn from all classes and must penetrate all classes (not only the working class), "dictating" to all classes; "dictating a positive program of action, alike to rebellious students, to dissatisfied Zemstvo figures [i.e., leaders of the rural liberal nobility], to discontented religious sectaries, to indignant school teachers, etc." (vol. V, p. 398). In short, it is to speak in the name of the working class; it is to use that numerous and closely packed class as its main battering ram in its struggle for power, but is itself to supply the doctrine, the watchwords, the purposes, the commands. It calls itself the "vanguard of the working class" because it brings to, nay injects into, the working class its own consciousness of that class's "historic mission." But it is to be, no less, the overseer for the whole of society, the "dictator of the program" of all classes of society. (In this bold, crude, repetitious hammering home of his ruthless doctrine, thus early can we discern the outlines of Lenin's future "dictatorship of the proletariat" over the proletariat and over society as a whole.)

5. Such a "party of a new type" needs an organization of a new type. It should be organized like an

army, have the unquestioning military discipline of an army, be centralized like an army, with all power and authority residing in its "general staff" or Central Committee. The Central Committee should plan, the local branches execute. The Central Committee should decide all general questions, the branches merely discuss how to grasp those decisions and carry them out. The Central Committee should have the right to form branches, dissolve them, purge them, appoint their leaders, eliminate, even exterminate, the unworthy (vol. V, p. 448; vol. VI, pp. 211–15 and 221–23; vol. VIII, pp. 365–66).

The workers, schooled by life in factory and barracks, would take naturally to this. They have no time for "the toy forms of democracy." Bureaucracy and centralism in organization are truly revolutionary; democracy in party matters, however, is "opportunism in the organization question."

This last epithet shows that for his new dogmas Lenin was creating new transgressions, which required new names. Among them was *khvostism* ("tailism," from Russian *khvost,* "a tail"), which meant that instead of directing, leading, pushing, and injecting your own purposes into the workers you seek merely to serve them and their purposes, hence "dragging at their tail." A kindred offense was "slavish kowtowing before spontaneity" (vol. V, pp. 350–58).

Rosa Luxemburg was offended in her whole being by Lenin's worship of centralism, his implicit contempt for the working class, its own creative impulses and purposes, and his distrust of all spontaneous developments and of spontaneity itself. It is here that her pamphlet joins issue with him.

Her polemical tone is, for her, remarkably gentle. She breaks a lance against his "pitiless" ultra-centralism. She rightly pictures his future party as one in which the Central Committee can and will perpetuate itself, dictate to the party, and have the party dictate to the masses. The Central Committee would "be the only thinking element," the entire party and the masses being reduced to mere "executing limbs." She reminds him how many times in recent history the masses had shown "spontaneous creativeness," surprising the party, making a mockery of its pedantic formulae and recipes. With a marvelous sensitivity to what is in the air (this is 1904 and the storms of 1905 are approaching), she predicts that the masses will soon take the party leaders by surprise once more, again showing their own multiform creativeness and again overflowing the narrow channels of party prescription.

She closes with a plea for the autonomy of the masses, respect for their spontaneity and creativeness, respect also for their right to make their own mistakes and be helped by them. Her polemic ends with the words, so often quoted: "Let us speak plainly. Historically, the errors committed by a truly revolutionary movement are infinitely more fruitful than the infallibility of the cleverest Central Committee."

THE RUSSIAN REVOLUTION

Nearly a quarter of a century passed. Lenin's party developed in the direction which Rosa Luxemburg had foreseen. In 1917, unexpectedly to all the socialist movements, the weak Tsar Nicholas II, having exhausted all social supports from grand dukes down, fell from power. For many months the real power was in the moods, whims, and will of millions of armed peasants in uniform, possessed by the idea of seizing the land, deserting the front, ending the war.

A Provisional Government arose, without any real apparatus of administration or enforcement, recognizing all the freedoms which Rosa believed in, but holding that Russia was not "ripe" for socialism and that the cruel war must somehow be continued until Russia was safe from the invader and a general peace arrived at.

The real power remained "in the streets." By extreme appeals to demagogy, and by use of his tightly disciplined armed conspiracy calling itself a party, Lenin in November 1917 was able to seize power "as easily as lifting up a feather" (Lenin, vol. XXVII, p. 76).

From her prison cell, on the basis of oral accounts from visitors and scraps of news in German and Russian newspapers smuggled into her cell, Rosa began a short, friendly, yet necessarily critical, appraisal of what was happening in Russia. She intended it for publication as one of her underground *Spartacus Letters*. The "Letter," like its author, was to have a tragic history.

The little pamphlet was never altogether finished. On November 9, 1918, a democratic revolution in Germany opened the doors of Rosa Luxemburg's prison. She stepped out into a world she had not made and found herself "at the head" of a movement which looked to her for leadership but, being drunk with the heady wine of Lenin's success, could no longer comprehend her voice nor follow her lead. They had been so "Russified" that her differences with them were now of the same order, if not the same magnitude, as her differences with Lenin. Yet because they considered her their responsible leader, she felt constrained to follow where they rushed.

In Germany elections were being held for a Constituent Assembly to write a new constitution for the new Germany. As a believer in democracy, she naturally assumed that her party (then calling itself *Spartakus* or the Spartacans) would contest these universal, democratic elections. But Lenin in Russia had dispersed by force of arms a democratically elected Constitutent Assembly, proclaiming instead a "Government of the Workers' and Soldiers' Councils"—in actual fact, a government of his party. Rosa's "followers" outvoted her, deciding to boycott the elections to the German Constituent Assembly and proclaim a "Government of the Workers' and Soldiers' Councils" of Germany. Her party dragged its reluctant leader in its wake.

A week after her release from prison, in the first issue of its new paper, *Rote Fahne* (dated Nov. 18, 1918), she made a solemn pledge to the masses: "The Spartacus League will never take over governmental power in any other way than through the clear, unambiguous will of the great majority of the proletarian masses in all Germany, never except by virtue of their conscious assent to the views, aims, and fighting methods of the Spartacus League."

But in the third week of December, "the masses," as represented in the First National Congress of the Councils of Workers' and Soldiers' Deputies, rejected by an overwhelming majority the Spartacan motion that the Councils should disrupt the Constituent Assembly and the Provisional Democratic Government and seize power themselves.

In the light of Rosa's public pledge, the duty of her movement seemed clear: to accept the decision, or to seek to have it reversed not by force but by persuasion. However, on the last two days of 1918 and the first day of 1919, the Spartacans held a convention of their own where they outvoted their "leader" once more. In vain she tried to convince them that to oppose both the Councils and the Constituent Assembly with their tiny forces was madness and a breaking of their democratic faith. They voted to try to take power in the streets, that is, by armed uprising. Almost alone in her party, Rosa Luxemburg decided with a heavy heart to lend her energy and her name to their effort.

The *Putsch*,[9] with inadequate forces and overwhelming mass disapproval except in Berlin, was, as she had predicted, a fizzle. But neither she nor her close associates fled for safety as Lenin had done in July 1917. They stayed in the capital, hiding carelessly in easily suspected hideouts, trying to direct an orderly retreat. On January 16, a little over two months after she had been released from prison, Rosa Luxemburg was seized, along with Karl Liebknecht and Wilhelm Pieck. Reactionary officers murdered Liebknecht and Luxemburg while "taking them to prison." Pieck was spared, to become, as the reader knows, one of the puppet rulers of Moscow-controlled East Germany today.

Leo Jogiches spent the next few days exposing the murder, until his arrest. He was taken to the Moabit Prison, where Radek, Lenin's emissary to the Spartacans and to any German forces which the

9 *Putsch* is a German term for a *coup d'état* attempted by a minority behind the backs or without the support of the majority of the people.

Russian ruler "might do business with," was also taken. On March 10 Jogiches was dragged out and murdered, but Radek, armored by investiture with a fragment of Lenin's governmental power, was permitted to sit in his cell, holding court for German officers and German heavy industrialists, as well as German Communists, and beginning the negotiations which led to the Reichswehr–Red Army secret military agreement, foreshadow of the future Stalin-Hitler Pact. In its way, the fate of the Russian emissary Radek and the "Russified" Pieck on the one hand, and that of Rosa Luxemburg on the other, are fitting symbols of the differences between Luxemburg's and Lenin's conceptions of the relationships between socialist principles and power.[10]

Rosa Luxemburg's little treatise on the Russian Revolution continued to have a pathetic career. The growing subordination of the Spartacan Movement, germ of the future Communist Party, to Lenin and Russian Communism caused her friends to suppress her work. They said that she had "lacked adequate information," that it was "untimely to publish it" (it is still "untimely" for them today!), nor did they scruple to say that she had "changed her mind" on her views of a lifetime as expressed in it.

---

10 For an account of the secret agreement initiated by Radek and von Seeckt, see G. Hilger and A. Meyer, *The Incompatible Allies* (New York, 1953); L. Kochan, *Russia and the Weimar Republic* (Cambridge, 1954); Gerald Freund, *Unholy Alliance* (New York, 1957); Hans W. Gatzke, "Russo-German Military Collaboration During the Weimar Republic," *The American Historical Review*, April, 1958, pp. 565–97.

When the censorship by her own comrades was at last broken, it was by one of her closest associates, Paul Levi. But he published the pamphlet only when he was breaking with Lenin and Leninism, out of disgust with another attempted *Putsch,* and disgust with Lenin, who secretly agreed with him but for reasons of political expediency publicly excoriated him for his open criticism of his party's errors. Zealous young Communists were told that he was violating Rosa Luxemburg's cherished wish to have it suppressed and that they would read it only at their soul's peril. The Social Democrats took it up, both in Germany and in France, where it was published in *Le Populaire* in 1922, but the Communists read only distorting commentaries and refutations. The unfortunate little classic was made a faction football and kicked around until it disappeared from view.

The disease which Rosa had foreseen as inseparable from a Russian and Lenin-dominated International did indeed infect the Comintern. As its "Stalinization" in the middle and late twenties extruded one group after another of the original founders, the Communist "splinter groups" thus arising felt the need of understanding the process of the decay of the Communist International from a supposed international association of brother parties into an agency of the Russian state, party, and dictator. Both Rosa's 1904 articles on the Leninist organization plan and her critical appraisal of the Russian Revolution were revived once more.

In the course of the thirties, *The Russian Revolution* was republished in German in Paris by an exile group called *Neuer Weg*; in French in a translation by Maurice Olivier; and sections of it in English, translated by Integer, were published in his *International Review* in New York. In 1928 the first textually scientific edition was published in German by Felix Weill of the Institut fuer Sozialforschung in Gruenberg's *Archiv fuer die Geschichte des Sozialismus und der Arbeiterbewegung*. It is this version, supplemented by a variorum study of all other versions in German, French, and English, which the author of the present introduction used in 1940 for a new English language translation, published then by the Workers Age Publishers (New York). That translation is used in the present edition.

HER APPRAISAL OF THE RUSSIAN REVOLUTION

All around her the Russian Revolution was regarded with blind hatred or blind idolatry. But in the darkness of her prison cell, in a land made doubly dark by war and by her movement's betrayal of its pledges, she did not let the light she thought she descried in the eastern sky blind her to the dangers inherent in Lenin's method of seizing and using power.

The great service of the Bolsheviks, she thought, was to have "put socialism on the order of the day," to have begun to feel for a way out of the shambles of war, to have redeemed the tarnished honor of international socialism. But this was no model revolution carried on under model laboratory conditions. It had occurred in the midst of war and alien invasion, in a backward land, cursed with poverty, lacking in a democratic tradition, ill-equipped economically and culturally for the building of a "higher" social order. "It would be a crazy idea to think that every last thing done and left undone under such abnormal conditions should represent the very pinnacle of perfection. . ."

SOCIALISM INSEPARABLE FROM DEMOCRACY

The heart of her pamphlet, as of her activities and teachings, lay in her unshakable belief in the initiative and capacity of the mass of mankind. That had been the real principle of her disagreement with Lenin in 1904 as it was two months before her death. To her the health-giving force of socialism was an attempt to extend democracy still further, to strengthen the pulse-beat of public life, to awaken hitherto inert masses to activity, to awareness of their own capacities for achievement and correction of their own errors, to initiative for the direct, popular solution of all problems, to the assumption of control over "their own" party, "their own" state machine, over industry, and over their own destinies.

There were more contradictory elements in her broad view than in Lenin's narrow authoritarian conception, for she knew too much of revolutions and was too much a revolutionary to reject the employment of a temporary dictatorship to defend the "new order" from overthrow by its yet existent enemies. But she regarded such dictatorship as an evil, even if under some circumstances a necessary one, an evil to be mitigated as much as possible by making it as temporary as possible and limiting its scope as far as possible, while offsetting its dictatorial potential by greatly extending its exact opposite and antidote, freedom. The one hope of preventing a degeneration of a revolution even in its victory lay, to her mind, in the simultaneous enormous extension of democracy and freedom to the widest possible number of human beings:

Freedom only for the supporters of the government, only for the members of one party—however numerous they may be—is no freedom at all. Freedom is always and exclusively freedom for the one who thinks differently. Not because of any fanatical concept of 'justice' but because all that is instructive, wholesome, and purifying in political freedom depends on this essential characteristic, and its effectiveness vanishes when 'freedom' becomes a special privilege.

Is there any regime which loves liberty which could not be proud to engrave these three sentences over the portals of its public buildings?

As a socialist, she wanted socialism introduced, but she knew that her ideal of socialism could not be introduced without the widest possible democracy and freedom. No party, she felt, had a monopoly of wisdom, or a filing cabinet full of ready-made solutions to the thousands of new problems that would present themselves in the course of carrying on an "old order" and still more in the course of trying to institute a "new." The actual solutions were to her neither a matter of authority nor prescription but of endless experiment, of fruitful trial and error, and fruitful correction of error. "Socialism by its very nature cannot be introduced by *ukaz* . . . Only unobstructed, effervescing life falls into a thousand new forms and improvisations, brings to light creative force, itself corrects all mistaken attempts."

Her "worship of spontaneity," her rejection of authoritarianism, were farther apart from Lenin's views than ever. The differences of 1904 had grown as the occasion for their expression had grown. How prophetic do her words sound now, forty-three years after they were written:

With the repression of political life in the land as a whole, life in the Soviets must also become more and more crippled. Without general elections, without unrestricted freedom of press and assembly, without a free struggle of opinions, life dies out in every public institution, becomes a mere semblance of life, in which only the bureaucracy remains the active element. Public life gradually falls asleep, a few dozen party leaders of inexhaustible energy and boundless experience direct and rule. Among them, in reality, only a dozen outstanding heads do the leading and an elite of the working class is invited from time to time to meetings where they are to applaud the speeches of the leaders, and to approve proposed resolutions unanimously—at bottom then, a clique affair—a dictatorship to be sure, not however of the proletariat but only of a handful of politicians . . . Such conditions must inevitably cause a brutalization of public life: attempted assassinations, shooting of hostages, etc.

Much of what Rosa Luxemburg wrote in this little pamphlet is now hopelessly dated, for much of it stems from dogmas which would not bear examination and have not resisted the passage of time. Yet how much of the forty-three years of subsequent Soviet development did she foresee in the darkness of her prison cell! How alive is her love of liberty, and her astonishing ability to put into memorable words that love of freedom! It is these qualities, along with her astonishing powers of foresight of where ruthless dictatorship would lead, that make her four-decade-old, unfinished pamphlet of more than merely biographical and historical interest. It is, as it has come to be widely recognized, a classic of that now vanished Marxism socialist movement in which she was so ardent a crusader.

THE RUSSIAN REVOLUTION

CHAPTER I

FUNDAMENTAL SIGNIFICANCE OF THE RUSSIAN REVOLUTION

THE Russian Revolution is the mightiest event of the World War. Its outbreak, its unexampled radicalism, its enduring consequences, constitute the clearest condemnation of the lying phrases which official Social-Democracy so zealously supplied at the beginning of the war as an ideological cover for German imperialism's campaign of conquest. I refer to the phrases concerning the mission of German bayonets, which were to overthrow Russian Czarism and free its oppressed peoples.

The mighty sweep of the revolution in Russia, the profound results which have transformed all class relationships, raised all social and economic problems, and, with the fatality of their own inner logic developed consistently from the first phase of the bourgeois republic to ever more advanced stages, finally reducing the fall of Czarism to the status of a mere minor episode—all these things show as plain as day that the freeing of Russia was not an achievement of the war and the military defeat of Czarism, not some service of "German bayonets in German fists," as the *Neue Zeit* under Kautsky's editorship once promised in an editorial. They show, on the contrary, that the freeing of Russia had its roots deep in the soil of its own land and was fully matured internally. The military adventure of German imperialism under the ideological blessing of German Social-Democracy did not bring about the revolution in Russia but only served to interrupt it at first, to postpone it for a while after its first stormy rising tide in the years 1911-13, and then, after its outbreak, created for it the most difficult and abnormal conditions.

Moreover, for every thinking observer, these developments are a decisive refutation of the doctrinaire theory which Kautsky shared with the Government Social-Democrats,[1] according to which Russia, as an economically backward and predominantly agrarian land, was supposed not to be ripe for social revolution and proletarian dictatorship. This theory, which regards only a *bourgeois* revolution as feasible in Russia, is also the theory of the opportunist wing of the Russian labor movement, of the so-called Mensheviks, under the experienced leadership of Axelrod and Dan. And from this conception follow the tactics of the coalition of the socialists in Russia with bourgeois liberalism. On this basic conception of the Russian Revolution, from which follow automatically their detailed positions on questions of tactics, both the Russian and the German opportunists find themselves in agreement with the German Government Socialists. According to the opinion of all three, the Russian Revolution should have called a halt at the stage which German imperialism in its conduct of the war

---

1   During the war the German Social-Democracy divided into three factions: the majority leadership, which openly supported and entered into the Imperial government; the Kautsky section, which declined responsibility for the conduct of the war but supplied many of the theoretical arguments for those who accepted such responsibility; and the section led by Rosa Luxemburg and Karl Liebknecht, which openly opposed the war and counterposed international solidarity and proletarian revolution to it.

had set as its noble task, according to the mythology of the German Social-Democracy, i.e., it should have stopped with the overthrow of Czarism. According to this view, if the revolution has gone beyond that point and has set as its task the dictatorship of the proletariat, this is simply a mistake of the radical wing of the Russian labor movement, the Bolsheviks. And all difficulties which the revolution has met with in its further course, and all disorders it has suffered, are pictured as purely a result of this fateful error.

Theoretically, this doctrine (recommended as the fruit of "Marxist thinking" by the *Vorwärts* of Stampfer and by Kautsky alike) follows from the original "Marxist" discovery that the socialist revolution is a national and, so to speak, a domestic affair in each modern country taken by itself. Of course, in the blue mists of abstract formulae, a Kautsky knows very well how to trace the world-wide economic connections of capital which make of all modern countries a single integrated organism. The problems of the Russian Revolution, moreover—since it is a product of international developments plus the agrarian question— cannot possibly be solved within the limits of bourgeois society.

Practically, this same doctrine represents an attempt to get rid of any responsibility for the course of the Russian Revolution, so far as that responsibility concerns the international, and especially the German, proletariat, and to deny the international connections of this revolution. It is not Russia's unripeness which has been proved by the events of the war and the Russian Revolution, but the unripeness of the German proletariat for the fulfillment of its historic tasks. And to make this fully clear is the first task of a critical examination of the Russian Revolution.

The fate of the revolution in Russia depended fully upon international events. That the Bolsheviks have based their policy entirely upon the world proletarian revolution is the clearest proof of their political far-sightedness and firmness of principle and of the bold scope of their policies. In it is visible the mighty advance which capitalist development has made in the last decade. The revolution of 1905-07 roused only a faint echo in Europe. Therefore, it had to remain a mere opening chapter. Continuation and conclusion were tied up with the further development of Europe.

Clearly, not uncritical apologetics but penetrating and thoughtful criticism is alone capable of bringing out the treasures of experiences and teachings. Dealing as we are with the very first experiment in proletarian dictatorship in world history (and one taking place at that under the hardest conceivable conditions, in the midst of the world-wide conflagration and chaos of the imperialist mass slaughter, caught in the coils of the most reactionary military power in Europe, and accompanied by the completest failure on the part of the international working class), it would be a crazy idea to think that every last thing done or left undone in an experiment with the dictatorship of the proletariat under such abnormal conditions represented the very pinnacle of perfection. On the contrary, elementary conceptions of socialist politics and an insight into their historically necessary prerequisites force us to understand that under such fatal conditions even the most gigantic idealism and the most storm-tested revolutionary energy are incapable of realizing democracy and socialism but only distorted attempts at either.

To make this stand out clearly in all its fundamental aspects and consequences is the elementary duty of the socialists of all countries; for only on the background of this bitter knowledge can we measure the enormous magnitude of the responsibility of the international proletariat itself for the fate of the Russian Revolution. Furthermore, it is only on this basis that the decisive importance of the resolute international action of the proletarian revolution can become effective, without which action as its necessary support, even the greatest energy and the greatest sacrifices of the proletariat in a single country must inevitably become tangled in a maze of contradiction and blunders.

There is no doubt either that the wise heads at the helm of the Russian Revolution, that Lenin and Trotsky on their thorny path beset by traps of all kinds, have taken many a decisive step only with the greatest inner hesitation and with most violent inner opposition. And surely nothing can be farther from their though ts than to believe that all the things they have done or left undone under the conditions of bitter compι lsion and necessity in the midst of the roaring whirlpool of events, should be regarded by the International as a shining example of socialist policy toward which only uncritical admiration and zealous imitation are in order.

It would be no less wrong to fear that a critical examination of the road so far taken by the Russian Revolution would serve to weaken the respect for and the attractive power of the example of the Russian Revolution, which alone can overcome the fatal inertia of the German masses. Nothing is farther from the truth. An awakening of the revolutionary energy of the working class in Germany can never again be called forth in the spirit of the guardianship methods of the German Social-Democracy of late-lamented memory. It can never again be conjured forth by any spotless authority, be it that of our own "higher committees" or that of "the Russian example." Not by the creation of a revolutionary hurrah-spirit, but quite the contrary: only by an insight into all the fearful seriousness, all the complexity of the tasks involved, only as a result of political maturity and independence of spirit, only as a result of a capacity for critical judgment on the part of the masses, which capacity was systematically killed by the Social-Democracy for decades under various pretexts, only thus can the genuine capacity for historical action be born in the German proletariat. To concern one's self with a critical analysis of the Russian Revolution in all its historical connections is the best training for the German and the international working class for the tasks which confront them as an outgrowth of the present situation.

The first period of the Russian Revolution, from its beginning in March to the October Revolution, corresponds exactly in its general outlines to the course of development of both the Great English Revolution and the Great French Revolution. It is the typical course of every first general reckoning of the revolutionary forces begotten within the womb of bourgeois society.

Its development moves naturally in an ascending line: from moderate beginnings to ever-greater radicalization of aims and, parallel with that, from a coalition of classes and parties to the sole rule of the radical party.

At the outset in March 1917, the "Cadets," that is the liberal bourgeoisie, stood at the head of the revo-

lution.[2] The first general rising of the revolutionary
tide swept every one and everything along with it.
The Fourth Duma, ultra-reactionary product of the
ultra-reactionary four-class right of suffrage and arising out of the *coup d'état,* was suddenly converted
into an organ of the revolution. All bourgeois parties,
even those of the nationalistic right, suddenly formed
a phalanx against absolutism. The latter fell at the
first attack almost without a struggle, like an organ
that had died and needed only to be touched to drop
off. The brief effort, too, of the liberal bourgeoisie to
save at least the throne and the dynasty collapsed
within a few hours. The sweeping march of events
leaped in days and hours over distances that formerly,
in France, took decades to traverse. In this, it became
clear that Russia was realizing the result of a century of European development, and above all, that
the revolution of 1917 was a direct continuation of
that of 1905-07, and not a gift of the German "lib-
erator." The movement of March 1917 linked itself
directly onto the point where, ten years earlier, its
work had broken off. The democratic republic was
the complete, internally ripened product of the very
first onset of the revolution.

Now, however, began the second and more difficult task. From the very first moment, the driving
force of the revolution was the mass of the urban
proletariat. However, its demands did not limit themselves to the realization of political democracy but
were concerned with the burning question of international policy—immediate peace. At the same time,
the revolution embraced the mass of the army, which
raised the same demand for immediate peace, and

---

2   *Cadets,* an abbreviation derived from the Russian ini-
tials of the party calling itself the Constitutional Democrats.

the mass of the peasants, who pushed the agrarian question into the foreground, that agrarian question which since 1905 had been the very axis of the revolution. Immediate peace and land—from these two aims the internal split in the revolutionary phalanx followed inevitably. The demand for immediate peace was in most irreconcilable opposition to the imperialist tendencies of the liberal bourgeoisie for whom Milyukov was the spokesman. On the other hand, the land question was a terrifying spectre for the other wing of the bourgeoisie, the rural landowners. And, in addition, it represented an attack on the sacred principle of private property in general, a touchy point for the entire propertied class.

Thus, on the very day after the first victories of the revolution, there began an inner struggle within it over the two burning questions—peace and land. The liberal bourgeoisie entered upon the tactics of dragging out things and evading them. The laboring masses, the army, the peasantry, pressed forward ever more impetuously. There can be no doubt that with the questions of peace and land, the fate of the political democracy of the republic was linked up. The bourgeois classes, carried away by the first stormy wave of the revolution, had permitted themselves to be dragged along to the point of republican government. Now they began to seek a base of support in the rear and silently to organize a counter-revolution. The Kaledin Cossack campaign against Petersburg was a clear expression of this tendency. Had the attack been successful, then not only the fate of the peace and land questions would have been sealed, but the fate of the republic as well. Military dictatorship, a reign of terror against the proletariat, and then return to monarchy, would have been the inevitable results.

From this we can judge the utopian and fundamentally reactionary character of the tactics by which the Russian "Kautskyans" or Mensheviks permitted themselves to be guided. Hardened in their addiction to the myth of the bourgeois character of the Russian Revolution—for the time being, you see, Russia is not supposed to be ripe for the social revolution!—they clung desperately to a coalition with the bourgeois liberals. But this means a union of elements which had been split by the natural internal development of the revolution and had come into the sharpest conflict with each other. The Axelrods and Dans wanted to collaborate at all costs with those classes and parties from which came the greatest threat of danger to the revolution and to its first conquest, democracy.

It is especially astonishing to observe how this industrious man (Kautsky), by his tireless labor of peaceful and methodical writing during the four years of the World War, has torn one hole after another in the fabric of socialism. It is a labor from which socialism emerges riddled like a sieve, without a whole spot left in it. The uncritical indifference with which his followers regard this industrious labor of their official theoretician and swallow each of his new discoveries without so much as batting an eyelash, finds its only counterpart in the indifference with which the followers of Scheidemann and Co. look on while the latter punch socialism full of holes in practise. Indeed, the two labors completely supplement each other. Since the outbreak of the war, Kautsky, the official guardian of the temple of Marxism, has really only been doing in theory the same things which the Scheidemanns have been doing in practise, namely: (1) the International an instrument of peace; (2) disarmament, the League of Nations and nationalism; and finally (3) democracy *not* socialism.[3]

In this situation, the Bolshevik tendency performs the historic service of having proclaimed from the very beginning, and having followed with iron con-

---

3   Here, as at various points in the manuscript, the passage is still in the form of rough notations which Rosa Luxemburg intended to expand and complete later. Her murder by military agents of the Social-Democratic coalition government prevented her from completing and revising the work. The expression, "the International an instrument of peace" refers to the excuses Kautsky gave for its bankruptcy during the war ("an instrument of peace is not suited to times of war"). It probably refers also to the theory that the International, being peaceful, is not an instrument for revolutionary struggle. Kautsky substituted utopian talk of disarmament (without the removal of the causes and roots of war!) for a revolutionary struggle against war. He provided apologetics for the League of Nations which was supposed to have banished war from the world. And he justified the socialists of each country when they abandoned internationalism, supported their own governments and ruling classes, and became in theory and practice nationalists instead of internationalists. When the struggle for socialism began in earnest, the Scheidemanns defended capitalism *against* socialism in practise, while Kautsky did so in theory by pretending that capitalist "democracy" was democracy in the abstract, and that they were defending "democracy." Hence the third point means: the advocacy of democracy *as against socialism.*

The passage in slightly expanded form might read something as follows:

"(1) the International as an instrument for peace-time only and for the maintenance of peace; (2) advocacy of the doctrines of disarmament, apologetics for the League of Nations and nationalism as against internationalism; (3) and the advocacy of "democracy" *as against* socialism.

sistency, those tactics which alone could save democracy and drive the revolution ahead. All power exclusively in the hands of the worker and peasant masses, in the hands of the soviets—this was indeed the only way out of the difficulty into which the revolution had gotten; this was the sword stroke with which they cut the Gordian knot, freed the revolution from a narrow blind-alley and opened up for it an untrammeled path into the free and open fields.

The party of Lenin was thus the only one in Russia which grasped the true interest of the revolution in that first period. It was the element that drove the revolution forward, and, thus it was the only party which really carried on a socialist policy.

It is this which makes clear, too, why it was that the Bolsheviks, though they were at the beginning of the revolution a persecuted, slandered and hunted minority attacked on all sides, arrived within the shortest time to the head of the revolution and were able to bring under their banner all the genuine masses of the people: the urban proletariat, the army, the peasants, as well as the revolutionary elements of democracy, the left wing of the Socialist-Revolutionaries.[4]

The real situation in which the Russian Revolution

---

4 The Socialist-Revolutionaries were a party made up largely of petty bourgeois and declassed intellectuals and peasants. It was not a Marxist party. Its program included the advocacy of a democratic revolution in Russia. When Rosa Luxemburg speaks here of the "revolutionary elements of democracy," she is referring to the left wing of the Socialist-Revolutionary party which joined with the Bolsheviks in the struggle for peace, the seizure of the land, and the transfer of power to the soviets. They later broke with the Bolsheviks, principally on the issue of the signing of the Brest-Litovsk Treaty.

found itself, narrowed down in a few months to the alternative: victory of the counter-revolution or dictatorship of the proletariat—Kaledin or Lenin. Such was the objective situation, just as it quickly presents itself in every revolution after the first intoxication is over, and as it presented itself in Russia as a result of the concrete, burning questions of peace and land, for which there was no solution within the framework of bourgeois revolution.

In this, the Russian Revolution has but confirmed the basic lesson of every great revolution, the law of its being, which decrees: either the revolution must advance at a rapid, stormy and resolute tempo, break down all barriers with an iron hand and place its goals ever farther ahead, or it is quite soon thrown backward behind its feeble point of departure and suppressed by counter-revolution. To stand still, to mark time on one spot, to be contented with the first goal it happens to reach, is never possible in revolution. And he who tries to apply the home-made wisdom derived from parliamentary battles between frogs and mice to the field of revolutionary tactics only shows thereby that the very psychology and laws of existence of revolution are alien to him and that all historical experience is to him a book sealed with seven seals.

Take the course of the English Revolution from its onset in 1642. There the logic of things made it necessary that the first feeble vacillations of the Presbyterians, whose leaders deliberately evaded a decisive battle with Charles I and victory over him, should inevitably be replaced by the Independents, who drove them out of Parliament and seized the power for themselves. And in the same way, within the army of the Independents, the lower petty-bourgeois mass of

the soldiers, the Lilburnian "Levellers" constituted
the driving force of the entire Independent movement; just as, finally, the proletarian elements within
the mass of the soldiers, the elements that went far-
thest in their aspirations for social revolution and who
found their expression in the Digger movement, constituted in their turn the leaven of the democratic
party of the "Levellers."

Without the moral influence of the revolutionary
proletarian elements on the general mass of the soldiers, without the pressure of the democratic mass
of the soldiers upon the bourgeois upper layers of the
party of the Independents, there would have been no
"purge" of the Long Parliament of its Presbyterians,
nor any victorious ending to the war with the army
of the Cavaliers and Scots, nor any trial and execution of Charles I, nor any abolition of the House of
Lords and proclamation of a republic.

And what happened in the Great French Revolution? Here, after four years of struggle, the seizure
of power by the Jacobins proved to be the only means
of saving the conquests of the revolution, of achieving
a republic, of smashing feudalism, of organizing a
revolutionary defense against inner as well as outer
foes, of suppressing the conspiracies of counter-revolution and spreading the revolutionary wave from
France to all Europe.

Kautsky and his Russian coreligionists who wanted
to see the Russian Revolution keep the "bourgeois
character" of its first phase, are an exact counterpart
of those German and English liberals of the preceding century who distinguished between the two
well-known periods of the Great French Revolution:
the "good" revolution of the first Girondin phase and
the "bad" one after the Jacobin uprising. The Liberal

shallowness of this conception of history, to be sure, doesn't care to understand that, without the uprising of the "immoderate" Jacobins, even the first, timid and half-hearted achievements of the Girondin phase would soon have been buried under the ruins of the revolution, and that the real alternative to Jacobin dictatorship—as the iron course of historical development posed the question in 1793—was not "moderate" democracy, but . . . restoration of the Bourbons! The "golden mean" cannot be maintained in any revolution. The law of its nature demands a quick decision: either the locomotive drives forward full steam ahead to the most extreme point of the historical ascent, or it rolls back of its own weight again to the starting point at the bottom; and those who would keep it with their weak powers half way up the hill, it but drags down with it irredeemably into the abyss.

Thus it is clear that in every revolution only that party is capable of seizing the leadership and power which has the courage to issue the appropriate watchwords for driving the revolution ahead, and the courage to draw all the necessary conclusions from the situation. This makes clear, too, the miserable role of the Russian Mensheviks, the Dans, Zeretellis, etc., who had enormous influence on the masses at the beginning, but, after their prolonged wavering and after they had fought with both hands and feet against taking over power and responsibility, were driven ignobly off the stage.

The party of Lenin was the only one which grasped the mandate and duty of a truly revolutionary party and which, by the slogan—"All power in the hands of the proletariat and peasantry"—insured the continued development of the revolution.

Thereby the Bolsheviks solved the famous problem of "winning a majority of the people," which problem has ever weighed on the German Social-Democracy like a nightmare. As bred-in-the-bone disciples of parliamentary cretinism,[5] these German Social-Democrats have sought to apply to revolutions the home-made wisdom of the parliamentary nursery: in order to carry anything, you must first have a majority. The same, they say, applies to revolution: first let's become a "majority." The true dialectic of revolutions, however, stands this wisdom of parliamentary moles on its head: not through a majority to revolutionary tactics, but through revolutionary tactics to a majority—that is the way the road runs.

Only a party which knows how to lead, that is, to advance things, wins support in stormy times. The determination with which, at the decisive moment, Lenin and his comrades offered the only solution which could advance things ("all power in the hands of the proletariat and peasantry"), transformed them almost overnight from a persecuted, slandered, outlawed minority whose leader had to hide like Marat in cellars, into the absolute master of the situation.

Moreover, the Bolsheviks immediately set as the aim of this seizure of power a complete, far-reaching revolutionary program: not the safeguarding of bourgeois democracy, but a dictatorship of the proletariat for the purpose of realizing socialism. Thereby they won for themselves the imperishable historic distinction of having for the first time proclaimed the

---

5 A term first applied by Marx to those parliamentarians who think that all history is decided by motions, votes and points of order in parliamentary debate.

final aim of socialism as the direct program of practical politics.

Whatever a party could offer of courage, revolutionary far-sightedness and consistency in an historic hour, Lenin, Trotsky and the other comrades have given in good measure. All the revolutionary honor and capacity which western Social-Democracy lacked was represented by the Bolsheviks. Their October uprising was not only the actual salvation of the Russian Revolution; it was also the salvation of the honor of international socialism.

CHAPTER II

THE BOLSHEVIK LAND POLICY

THE Bolsheviks are the historic heirs of the English Levellers and the French Jacobins. But the concrete task which faced them after the seizure of power was incomparably more difficult than that of their historical predecessors. (Importance of the agrarian question. Even in 1905. Then, in the Third Duma, the right-wing peasants! The peasant question and defense, the army.[6])

Surely the solution of the problem by the direct, immediate seizure and distribution of the land by the peasants was the shortest, simplest, most clean-cut formula to achieve two diverse things: to break down large land-ownership, and immediately to bind the peasants to the revolutionary government. As a political measure to fortify the proletarian socialist government, it was an excellent tactical move. Unfortunately, however, it had two sides to it; and the reverse side consisted in the fact that the direct seizure of the land by the peasants has in general nothing at all in common with socialist economy.

A socialist transformation of economic relationships

---

6 Here, as in a number of other places, the manuscript consists only of rough notes which Rosa Luxemburg intended to expand later. As the meaning of these passages is in general clear, I have preferred to translate them literally, just as the author left them.

presupposes two things so far as agrarian relationships are concerned:

In the first place, only the nationalization of the large landed estates, as the technically most advanced and most concentrated means and methods of agrarian production, can serve as the point of departure for the socialist mode of production on the land. Of course, it is not necessary to take away from the small peasant his parcel of land, and we can with confidence leave him to be won over voluntarily by the superior advantages of social production and to be persuaded of the advantages first of union in cooperatives and then finally of inclusion in the general socialized economy as a whole. Still, every socialist economic reform on the land must obviously begin with large and medium land-ownership. Here the property right must first of all be turned over to the nation, or to the state, which, with a socialist government, amounts to the same thing; for it is this alone which affords the possibility of organizing agricultural production in accord with the requirements of interrelated, large-scale socialist production.

Moreover, in the second place, its is one of the prerequisites of this transformation, that the separation between rural economy and industry which is so characteristic of bourgeois society, should be ended in such a way as to bring about a mutual interpenetration and fusion of both, to clear the way for the planning of both agrarian and industrial production according to a unified point of view. Whatever individual form the practical economic arrangements may take—whether through urban communes, as some propose, or directed from a governmental center— in any event, it must be preceded by a reform introduced from the center, and that in turn must be preceded by the nationalization of the land. The nationalization of the large and middle-sized estates and the union of industry and agriculture—these are two fundamental requirements of any socialist economic reform, without which there is no socialism.

That the Soviet government in Russia has not carried through these mighty reforms—who can reproach them for that! It would be a sorry jest indeed to demand or expect of Lenin and his comrades that, in the brief period of their rule, in the center of the gripping whirlpool of domestic and foreign struggles, ringed about by countless foes and opponents—to expect that under such circumstances they should already have solved, or even tackled, one of the most difficult tasks, indeed, we can safely say, *the* most difficult task of the socialist transformation of society! Even in the West, under the most favorable conditions, once we have come to power, we too will break many a tooth on this hard nut before we are out of the worst of the thousands of complicated difficulties of this gigantic task!

A socialist government which has come to power must in any event do one thing: it must take measures which lead in the direction of that fundamental prerequisite for a later socialist reform of agriculture; it must at least avoid everything which may bar the way to those measures.

Now the slogan launched by the Bolsheviks, immediate seizure and distribution of the land by the peasants, necessarily tended in the opposite direction. Not only is it not a socialist measure; it even cuts off the way to such measures; it piles up insurmountable obstacles to the socialist transformation of agrarian relations.

The seizure of the landed estates by the peasants

according to the short and precise slogan of Lenin and his friends—*"Go and take the land for yourselves"*—simply led to the sudden, chaotic conversion of large landownership into peasant landownership. What was created is not social property but a new form of private property, namely, the breaking up of large estates into medium and small estates, or relatively advanced large units of production into primitive small units which operate with technical means from the time of the Pharaohs.

Nor is that all! Through these measures and the chaotic and purely arbitrary manner of their execution, differentiation in landed property, far from being eliminated, was even further sharpened. Although the Bolsheviks called upon the peasantry to form peasant committees so that the seizure of the nobles estates might, in some fashion, be made into a collective act, yet it is clear that this general advice could not change anything in the real practise and real relations of power on the land. With or without committees, it was the rich peasants and usurers who made up the village bourgeoisie possessing the actual power in their hands in every Russian village, that surely became the chief beneficiaries of the agrarian revolution. Without being there to see, any one can figure out for himself that in the course of the distribution of the land, social and economic inequality among the peasants was not eliminated but rather increased, and that class antagonisms were further sharpened. This shift of power, however, took place to the *disadvantage* of the interests of the proletariat and of socialism. Formerly, there was only a small caste of noble and capitalist landed proprietors and a small minority of rich village bourgeosie to oppose a socialist reform on the land. And their expropriation by a revolutionary mass movement of the people is mere child's play. But now, after the "seizure," as an opponent of any attempt at socialization of agrarian production, there is an enormous, newly developed and powerful mass of owning peasants who will defend their newly won property with tooth and nail against every socialist attack. The question of the future socialization of agrarian economy--that is, any socialization of production in general in Russia—has now become a question of opposition and of struggle between the urban proletariat and the mass of the peasantry. How sharp this antagonism has already become is shown by the peasant boycott of the cities, in which they withhold the means of existence to carry on speculation in them, in quite the same way as the Prussian Junker does.

The French small peasant became the boldest defender of the Great French Revolution which had given him land confiscated from the *emigrés*. As Napoleonic soldier, he carried the banner of France to victory, crossed all Europe and smashed feudalism to pieces in one land after another. Lenin and his friends might have expected a similar result from their agrarian slogan. However, now that the Russian peasant has seized the land with his own fist, he does not even dream of defending Russia and the revolution to which he owes the land. He has dug obstinately into his new possessions and abandoned the revolution to its enemies, the state to decay, the urban population to famine.

(Lenin's speech on the necessity of centralization in industry, nationalization of banks, of trade and of industry. Why not of the land? Here, on the contrary, decentralization and private property.

(Lenin's own agrarian program before the revolution was different. The slogan taken over from the much condemned Socialist-Revolutionaries, or rather, from the spontaneous peasant movement.

(In order to introduce socialist principles into agrarian relations, the Soviet government now seeks to create agrarian communes out of proletarians, mostly city unemployed. But it is easy to see in advance that the results of these efforts must remain so insignificant as to disappear when measured against the whole scope of agrarian relations. After the most appropriate starting points for socialist economy, the large estates, have been broken up into small units, now they are trying to build up communist model production units out of petty beginnings. Under the circumstances these communes can claim to be considered only as experiments and not as a general social reform. Grain monopoly with bounties. Now, *post-festum,* they want to introduce the class war into the village![7])

The Leninist agrarian reform has created a new and powerful layer of popular enemies of socialism on the countryside, enemies whose resistance will be much more dangerous and stubborn than that of the noble large landowners.

---

7 Here again the matter in parenthesis was to have been expanded by the author in completing the pamphlet.

CHAPTER III

THE NATIONALITIES QUESTION

THE Bolsheviks are in part responsible for the fact that the military defeat was transformed into the collapse and breakdown of Russia. Moreover, the Bolsheviks themselves have, to a great extent, sharpened the objective difficulties of this situation by a slogan which they placed in the foreground of their policies: the so-called right of self-determination of peoples, or —something which was really implicit in this slogan —the disintegration of Russia.

The formula of the right of the various nationalities of the Russian Empire to determine their fate independently "even to the point of the right of governmental separation from Russia," was proclaimed again with doctrinaire obstinacy as a special battle cry of Lenin and his comrades during their opposition against Miliukovist, and then Kerenskyan imperialism.[8] It constituted the axis of their inner policy after the October Revolution also. And it constituted the entire platform of the Bolsheviks at Brest-Litovsk,

---

8. The governments of Miliukov and Kerensky were two regimes preceding that of the Bolsheviks during the earlier months of 1917, after the downfall of the Czar. Both of these governments attempted to continue the war for the imperialist objectives of the old Russian Empire and denied the right of the national minorities to separation from Russia.

all they had to oppose to the display of force by German imperialism.[9]

One is immediately struck with the obstinacy and rigid consistency with which Lenin and his comrades stuck to this slogan, a slogan which is in sharp contradiction to their otherwise outspoken centralism in politics as well as to the attitude they have assumed towards other democratic principles. While they showed a quite cool contempt for the Constituent Assembly, universal suffrage, freedom of press and assemblage, in short, for the whole apparatus of the basic democratic liberties of the people which, taken all together, constituted the "right of self-determination" inside Russia, they treated the right of self-determination of peoples as a jewel of democratic policy for the sake of which all practical considerations of real criticism had to be stilled. While they did not permit themselves to be imposed upon in the slightest by the plebiscite for the Constituent Assembly in Russia, a plebiscite on the basis of the most democratic suffrage in the world, carried out in the full freedom of a popular republic, and while they simply declared this plebiscite null and void on the basis of a very sober evaluation of its results, still they championed the "popular vote" of the foreign nationalities of Russia on the question of which land they wanted to belong to, as the true palladium of all freedom and democracy, the unadulterated quintessence of the will of the peoples and as the court of last resort in questions of the political fate of nations.

The contradiction that is so obvious here is all the

9.   Brest-Litovsk was the town in which the representatives of Soviet Russia conducted peace negotiations with the representatives of Germany early in 1918.

harder to understand since the democratic forms of political life in each land, as we shall see, actually involve the most valuable and even indispensable foundations of socialist policy, whereas the famous "right of self-determination of nations" is nothing but hollow, petty-bourgeois phraseology and humbug.

Indeed, what is this right supposed to signify? It belongs to the ABC of socialist policy that socialism opposes every form of oppression, including also that of one nation by another.

If, despite all this, such generally sober and critical politicians as Lenin and Trotsky and their friends, who have nothing but an ironical shrug for every sort of utopian phrase such as disarmament, league of nations, etc., have in this case made a hollow phrase of exactly the same kind into their special hobby, this arose, it seems to us, as a result of some kind of policy made to order for the occasion. Lenin and his comrades clearly calculated that there was no surer method of binding the many foreign peoples within the Russian Empire to the cause of the revolution, to the cause of the socialist proletariat, than that of offering them, in the name of the revolution and of socialism, the most extreme and most unlimited freedom to determine their own fate. This was analogous to the policy of the Bolsheviks towards the Russian peasants, whose land-hunger was satisfied by the slogan of direct seizure of the noble estates and who were supposed to be bound thereby to the banner of the revolution and the proletarian government. In both cases, unfortunately, the calculation was entirely wrong.

While Lenin and his comrades clearly expected that, as champions of national freedom even to the extent of "separation," they would turn Finland, the

Ukraine, Poland, Lithuania, the Baltic countries, the Caucasus, etc., into so many faithful allies of the Russian Revolution, we have witnessed the opposite spectacle. One after another, these "nations" used the freshly granted freedom to ally themselves with German imperialism against the Russian Revolution as its mortal enemy, and, under German protection, to carry the banner of counter-revolution into Russia itself. The little game with the Ukraine at Brest, which caused a decisive turn of affairs in those negotiations and brought about the entire inner and outer political situation at present prevailing for the Bolsheviks, is a perfect case in point. The conduct of Finland, Poland, Lithuania, the Baltic lands, the peoples of the Caucasus, shows most convincingly that we are not dealing here with an exceptional case, but with a typical phenomenon.

To be sure, in all these cases, it was really not the "people" who engaged in these reactionary policies, but only the bourgeois and petty-bourgeois classes, who—in sharpest opposition to their own proletarian masses—perverted the "national right of self-determination" into an instrument of their counter-revolutionary class policies. But—and here we come to the very heart of the question—it is in this that the utopian, petty-bourgeois character of this nationalistic slogan resides: that in the midst of the crude realities of class society and when class antagonisms are sharpened to the uttermost, it is simply converted into a means of bourgeois class rule. The Bolsheviks were to be taught to their own great hurt and that of the revolution, that under the rule of capitalism there is no self-determination of peoples, that in a class society each class of the nation strives to "determine itself" in a different fashion, and that, for the bourgeois classes, the standpoint of national freedom is fully subordinated to that of class rule. The Finnish bourgeoisie, like the Ukrainian bourgeoisie, were unanimous in preferring the violent rule of Germany to national freedom, if the latter should be bound up with Bolshevism.

The hope of transforming these actual class relationships somehow into their opposite and of getting a majority vote for union with the Russian Revolution by depending on the revolutionary masses—if it was seriously meant by Lenin and Trotsky—represented an incomprehensible degree of optimism. And if it was only meant as a tactical flourish in the duel with the German politics of force, then it represented dangerous playing with fire. Even without German military occupation, the famous "popular plebiscite," supposing that it had come to that in the border states, would have yielded a result, in all probability, which would have given the Bolsheviks little cause for rejoicing; for we must take into consideration the psychology of the peasant masses and of great sections of the petty bourgeoisie, and the thousand ways in which the bourgeoisie could have influenced the vote. Indeed, it can be taken as an unbreakable rule in these matters of plebiscites on the national question that the ruling class will either know how to prevent them where it doesn't suit their purpose, or where they somehow occur, will know how to influence their results by all sorts of means, big and little, the same means which make it impossible to introduce socialism by a popular vote.

The mere fact that the question of national aspirations and tendencies towards separation were injected at all into the midst of the revolutionary struggle, and were even pushed into the foreground and made into the shibboleth of socialist and revolutionary policy as a result of the Brest peace, has served to bring the greatest confusion into socialist ranks and has actually destroyed the position of the proletariat in the border countries.

In Finland, so long as the socialist proletariat fought as a part of the closed Russian revolutionary phalanx, it possessed a position of dominant power: it had the majority in the Finnish parliament, in the army; it had reduced its own bourgeoisie to complete impotence, and was master of the situation within its borders.

Or take the Ukraine. At the beginning of the century, before the tomfoolery of "Ukrainian nationalism" with its silver rubles and its "Universals"[10] and Lenin's hobby of an "independent Ukraine" had been invented, the Ukraine was the stronghold of the Russian revolutionary movement. From there, from Rostov, from Odessa, from the Donetz region, flowed out the first lava-streams of the revolution (as early as 1902-04) which kindled all South Russia into a sea of flame, thereby preparing the uprising of 1905. The same thing was repeated in the present revolution, in which the South Russian proletariat supplied the picked troops of the proletarian phalanx. Poland and the Baltic lands have been since 1905 the mightiest and most dependable hearths of revolution, and in them the socialist proletariat has played an outstanding role.

How does it happen then that in all these lands the

---

10. The manuscript speaks of *Karbowentzen,* which I take to be a Germanization of the Russian word for "silver ruble," probably referring to a special Ukrainian coinage, and of *"Universals,"* the name applied to certain manifestoes or declarations of the Ukrainian Rada (national assembly).

counter-revolution suddenly triumphs? The nationalist movement, just because it tore the proletariat
loose from Russia, crippled it thereby, and delivered
it into the hands of the bourgeoisie of the border
countries.

Instead of acting in the same spirit of genuine
international class policy which they represented in
other matters, instead of working for the most com-
pact union of the revolutionary forces throughout
the area of the Empire, instead of defending tooth
and nail the integrity of the Russian Empire as an
area of revolution and opposing to all forms of separatism the solidarity and inseparability of the proletarians in all lands within the sphere of the Russian
Revolution as the highest command of politics, the
Bolsheviks, by their hollow nationalistic phraseology
concerning the "right of self-determination to the
point of separation," have accomplished quite the
contrary and supplied the bourgeoisie in all border
states with the finest, the most desirable pretext, the
very banner of the counter-revolutionary efforts. Instead of warning the proletariat in the border countries against all forms of separatism as mere bourgeois traps, they did nothing but confuse the masses
in all the border countries by their slogan and delivered them up to the demagogy of the bourgeois
classes. By this nationalistic demand they brought on
the disintegration of Russia itself, pressed into the
enemy's hand the knife which it was to thrust into the
heart of the Russian Revolution.

To be sure, without the help of German imperialism, without "the German rifle butts in German fists,"
as Kautsky's *Neue Zeit* put it, the Lubinskys and
other little scoundrels of the Ukraine, the Erichs and
Mannerheims of Finland, and the Baltic barons,

would never have gotten the better of the socialist masses of the workers in their respective lands. But national separatism was the Trojan horse inside which the German "comrades," bayonet in hand, made their entrance into all those lands. The real class antagonisms and relations of military force brought about German intervention. But the Bolsheviks provided the ideology which masked this campaign of counter-revolution; they strengthened the position of the bourgeoisie and weakened that of the proletariat.

The best proof is the Ukraine, which was to play so frightful a role in the fate of the Russian Revolution. Ukrainian nationalism in Russia was something quite different from, let us say, Czechish, Polish or Finnish nationalism in that the former was a mere whim, a folly of a few dozen petty-bourgeois intellectuals without the slightest roots in the economic, political or psychological relationships of the country; it was without any historical tradition, since the Ukraine never formed a nation or government, was without any national culture, except for the reactionary-romantic poems of Shevschenko. It is exactly as if, one fine day, the people living in the *Wasserkante*[11] should want to found a new Low-German (*Plattdeutsche*) nation and government! And this ridiculous pose of a few university professors and students was inflated into a political force by Lenin and his comrades through their doctrinaire agitation concerning the "right of self-determination including etc." To what was at first a mere farce they lent such importance that the farce became a matter of the most deadly seriousness—not as a serious national movement for

---

11. A region in Germany where the German dialect known as *Plattdeutsch* is spoken.

which, afterward as before, there are no roots at all, but as a shingle and rallying flag of counter-revolution! At Brest, out of this addled egg crept the German bayonets.

There are times when such phrases have a very real meaning in the history of class struggles. It is the unhappy lot of socialism that in this World War it was given to it to supply the ideological screens for counter-revolutionary policy. At the outbreak of the war, German Social-Democracy hastened to deck the predatory expedition of German imperialism with an ideological shield from the lumber-room of Marxism by declaring it to be a liberating expedition against Russian Czarism, such as our old teachers (Marx and Engels) had longed for. And to the lot of the Bolsheviks, who were the very antipodes of our government socialists, did it fall to supply grist for the mill of counter-revolution with their phrases about self-determination of peoples; and thereby to supply not alone the ideology for the strangling of the Russian Revolution itself, but even for the plans for settling the entire crisis arising out of the World War.

We have good reason to examine very carefully the policies of the Bolsheviks in this regard. The "right of self-determination of peoples," coupled with the league of nations and disarmament by the grace of President Wilson, constitute the battle-cry under which the coming reckoning of international socialism with the bourgeoisie is to be settled. It is obvious that the phrases concerning self-determination and the entire nationalist movement, which at present constitute the greatest danger for international socialism, have experienced an extraordinary strengthening from the Russian Revolution and the Brest negotiations. We shall yet have to go into this platform thoroughly. The tragic fate of these phrases in the Russian Revolution, on the thorns of which the Bolsheviks were themselves destined to be caught and bloodily scratched, must serve the international proletariat as a warning and lesson.

And from all this there followed the dictatorship of Germany from the time of the Brest treaty to the time of the "supplementary treaty." The two hundred expiatory sacrifices in Moscow. From this situation arose the terror and the suppression of democracy.[12]

12. Six weeks after. the signing of the Brest-Litovsk treaty, there was a codicil or supplement signed. The "two hundred expiatory sacrifices" may refer to the execution of persons charged with complicity in the assassination of tne German ambassador, Count von Mirbach. He was shot by terrorists of the Socialist-Revolutionary party, which had cooperated with the Bolsheviks until the signing of the Brest treaty and then went into opposition and tried to prevent the signing of the treaty. From then on, the Russian government was a one-party government.

CHAPTER IV

THE CONSTITUENT ASSEMBLY

L ET us test this matter further by taking a few examples.

The well-known dissolution of the Constituent Assembly in November 1917 played an outstanding role in the policy of the Bolsheviks. This measure was decisive for their further position; to a certain extent, it represented a turning point in their tactics.

It is a fact that Lenin and his comrades were stormily demanding the calling of a Constituent Assembly up to the time of their October victory, and that the policy of dragging out this matter on the part of the Kerensky government constituted an article in the indictment of that government by the Bolsheviks and was the basis of some of their most violent attacks upon it. Indeed, Trotsky says in his interesting pamphlet, *From October to Brest-Litovsk,* that the October Revolution represented "the salvation of the Constituent Assembly" as well as of the revolution as a whole. "And when we said," he continues, "that the entrance to the Constituent Assembly could not be reached through the Preliminary Parliament of Zeretelli, but only through the seizure of power by the Soviets, we were entirely right."

And then, after these declarations, Lenin's first step after the October Revolution was . . . the dissolution of this same Constituent Assembly, to which it was

supposed to be an entrance.[13] What reasons could be
decisive for so astonishing a turn? Trotsky, in the
above-mentioned pamphlet, discusses the matter
thoroughly, and we will set down his argument here:

"While the months preceding the October Revolution were a time of leftward movement on the part
of the masses and of an elemental flow of workers,
soldiers and peasants towards the Bolsheviks, inside
the Socialist-Revolutionary Party this process expressed itself as a strengthening of the left wing at
the cost of the right. But within the list of party can-
didates of the Socialist-Revolutionaries, the old names
of the right wing still occupied three fourths of the
places. . . .

"Then there was the further circumstance that the
elections themselves took place in the course of the
first weeks after the October Revolution. The news of
the change that had taken place spread rather slowly
in concentric circles from the capital to the provinces
and from the towns to the villages. The peasant
masses in many places had little notion of what went
on in Petrograd and Moscow. They voted for 'Land
and Freedom,' and elected as their representatives in
the land committees those who stood under the banner of the 'Narodniki.'[14] Thereby, however, they
voted for Kerensky and Avksentiev, who had been
dissolving these land committees and having their
members arrested. . . . This state of affairs gives a
clear idea of the extent to which the Constituent
Assembly had lagged behind the development of the

13. The Constituent Assembly was dissolved at its first
session in January 1918.

14. "Populists," a name used at this time for the Socialist-Revolutionary Party, which, as a party, supported
Kerensky and opposed the October Revolution.

political struggle and the development of party groupings."

All of this is very fine and quite convincing. But
one cannot help wondering how such clever people
as Lenin and Trotsky failed to arrive at the conclusion which follows immediately from the above facts.
Since the Constituent Assembly was elected long before the decisive turning point, the October Revolution,[15] and its composition reflected the picture of
the vanished past and not of the new state of affairs,
then it follows automatically that the outgrown and
therefore still-born Constituent Assembly should have
been annulled, and without delay, new elections to a
new Constituent Assembly should have been arranged.
They did not want to entrust, nor should they have
entrusted, the fate of the revolution to an assemblage
which reflected the Kerenskyan Russia of yesterday,
of the period of vacillations and coalition with the
bourgeoisie. Hence there was nothing left to do except
to convoke an assembly that would issue forth out of
the renewed Russia that had advanced further.

Instead of this, from the special inadequacy of the
Constituent Assembly which came together in October, Trotsky draws a general conclusion concerning
the inadequacy of any popular representation whatsoever which might come from universal popular elections during the revolution.

"Thanks to the open and direct struggle for governmental power," he writes, "the laboring masses
acquire in the shortest time an accumulation of political experience, and they climb rapidly from step to

15. Rosa Luxemburg is not correct: the elections for
the Constituent Assembly were largely arranged for prior
to the October Revolution but actually took place immediately after that event.

step in their political development. The bigger the country and the more rudimentary its technical apparatus, the less is the cumbersome mechanism of democratic institutions able to keep pace with this development."

Here we find the "mechanism of democratic institutions" as such called in question. To this we must at once object that in such an estimate of representative institutions there lies a somewhat rigid and schematic conception which is expressly contradicted by the historical experience of every revolutionary epoch. According to Trotsky's theory, every elected assembly reflects once and for all only the mental composition, political maturity and mood of its electorate just at the moment when the latter goes to the polling place. According to that, a democratic body is the reflection of the masses at the end of the electoral period, much as the heavens of Herschel always show us the heavenly bodies not as they are when we are looking at them but as they were at the moment they sent out their light-messages to the earth from the measureless distances of space. Any living mental connection between the representatives, once they have been elected, and the electorate, any permanent interaction between one and the other, is hereby denied.

Yet how all historical experience contradicts this! Experience demonstrates quite the contrary: namely, that the living fluid of the popular mood continuously flows around the representative bodies, penetrates them, guides them. How else would it be possible to witness, as we do at times in every bourgeois parliament, the amusing capers of the "people's representatives," who are suddenly inspired by a new "spirit" and give forth quite unexpected sounds; or to find the most dried-out mummies at times comporting themselves like youngsters and the most diverse little *Scheidemaennchen*[16] suddenly finding revolutionary tones in their breasts—whenever there is rumbling in factories and workshops and on the streets?

And is this ever-living influence of the mood and degree of political ripeness of the masses upon the elected bodies to be renounced in favor of a rigid scheme of party emblems and tickets in the very midst of revolution? Quite the contrary! It is precisely the revolution which creates by its glowing heat that delicate, vibrant, sensitive political atmosphere in which the waves of popular feeling, the pulse of popular life, work for the moment on the representative bodies in most wonderful fashion. It is on this very fact, to be sure, that the well-known moving scenes depend which invariably present themselves in the first stages of every revolution, scenes in which old reactionaries or extreme moderates, who have issued out of a parliamentary election by limited suffrage under the old regime, suddenly become the heroic and stormy spokesmen of the uprising. The classic example is provided by the famous "Long parliament" in England, which was elected and assembled in 1642 and remained at its post for seven whole years and reflected in its internal life all alterations and displacements of popular feeling, of political ripeness, of class differentiation, of the progress of the revolution to its highest point, from the initial devout skirmishes with the Crown under a Speaker who remained on his knees, to the abolition of the House of Lords, the execution of Charles and the proclamation of the republic.

---

16. "Little Scheidemen," a play on the name of the pro-war, government Social-Democrat, Phillip Scheidemann.

And was not the same wonderful transformation repeated in the French Estates General, in the censorship-subjected parliament of Louis Phillipe, and even —and this last, most striking example was very close to Trotsky—even in the Fourth Russian Duma which, elected in the Year of Grace 1909 under the most rigid rule of the counter-revolution, suddenly felt the glowing heat of the impending overturn and became the point of departure for the revolution?[17]

All this shows that "the cumbersome mechanism of democratic institutions" possesses a powerful corrective—namely, the living movement of the masses, their unending pressure. And the more democratic the institutions, the livelier and stronger the pulse-beat of the political life of the masses, the more direct and complete is their influence—despite rigid party banners, outgrown tickets (electoral lists), etc. To be sure, every democratic institution has its limits and shortcomings, things which it doubtless shares with all other human institutions. But the remedy which Trotsky and Lenin have found, the elimination of democracy as such, is worse than the disease it is supposed to cure; for it stops up the very living source from which alone can come the correction of all the innate shortcomings of social institutions. That source is the active, untrammeled, energetic political life of the broadest masses of the people.

---

17. It was this Fourth Duma which, after popular demonstrations in February 1917, sent two emissaries to the Czar to request his abdication.

CHAPTER V

THE QUESTION OF SUFFRAGE

L ET's take another striking example: the right of suffrage as worked out by the Soviet government. It is not altogether clear what practical significance is attributed to this right of suffrage. From the critique of democratic institutions by Lenin and Trotsky, it appears that popular representation on the basis of universal suffrage is rejected by them on principle, and that they want to base themselves only on the soviets. Why, then, any general suffrage system was worked out at all is really not clear. It is also not known to us whether this right of suffrage was put in practise anywhere,; nothing has been heard of any elections to any kind of popular representative body on the basis of it. More likely, it is only a theoretical product, so to speak, of diplomacy; but, as it is, it constitutes a remarkable product of the Bolshevist theory of dictatorship.

Every right of suffrage, like any political right in general, is not to be measured by some sort of abstract scheme of "justice," or in terms of any other bourgeois-democratic phrases, but by the social and economic relationships for which it is designed. The right of suffrage worked out by the Soviet government is calculated for the transition period from the bourgeois-capitalist to the socialist form of society, that is, it is calculated for the period of the proletarian dictatorship. But, according to the interpretation of this dictatorship which Lenin and Trotsky represent, the right to vote is granted only to those who live by their own labor and is denied to everybody else.

Now it is clear that such a right to vote has meaning only in a society which is in a position to make possible for all who want to work an adequate civilized life on the basis of one's own labor. Is that the case in Russia at present? Under the terrific difficulties which Russia has to contend with, cut off as she is from the world market and from her most important sources of raw materials, and under circumstances involving a terrific general uprooting of economic life and a rude overturn of productive relationships as a result of the transformation of property relationships in land and industry and trade--under such circumstances, it is clear that countless existences are quite suddenly uprooted, derailed without any objective possibility of finding any employment for their labor power within the economic mechanism. This applies not only to the capitalist and land-owning classes, but to the broad layer of the middle class also, and even to the working class itself. It is a known fact that the contraction of industry has resulted in a mass-scale return of the urban proletariat to the open country in search of a place in rural economy. Under such circumstances, a political right of suffrage on the basis of a general obligation to labor, is a quite incomprehensible measure. According to the main trend, only the exploiters are supposed to be deprived of their political rights. And, on the other hand, at the same time that productive labor powers are being uprooted on a mass scale, the Soviet government is often compelled to hand over national industry to its former owners, on lease, so to speak. In the same way, the Soviet government was forced to conclude a compromise with the bourgeois consumers cooperatives also. Further, the use of bourgeois specialists proved unavoidable. Another consequence of the same situation is that growing sections of the proletariat are maintained by the state out of public resources as Red Guardists, etc. In reality, broad and growing sections of the petty bourgeoisie and proletariat, for whom the economic mechanism provides no means of exercising the obligation to work, are rendered politically without any rights.

It makes no sense to regard the right of suffrage as a utopian product of fantasy, cut loose from social reality. And it is for this reason that it is not a serious instrument of the proletarian dictatorship. It is an anachronism, an anticipation of the juridical situation which is proper on the basis of an already completed socialist economy, but not in the transition period of the proletarian dictatorship.

As the entire middle class, the bourgeois and petty-bourgeois intelligentsia, boycotted the Soviet government for months after the October Revolution and crippled the railroad, post and telegraph, and educational and administrative apparatus, and, in this fashion, opposed the workers government, naturally enough all measures of pressure were exerted against it. These included the deprivation of political rights, of economic means of existence, etc., in order to break their resistance with an iron fist. It was precisely in this way that the socialist dictatorship expressed itself, for it cannot shrink from any use of force to secure or prevent certain measures involving the interests of the whole. But when it comes to a suffrage law which provides for the general disfranchisement of broad sections of society, whom it places politically outside the framework of society and, at the same time, is not

in a position to make any place for them even economically within that framework, when it involves
a deprivation of rights not as a concrete measure for
a concrete purpose but as a general rule of long-
standing effect, then it is not a necessity of dictatorship but a makeshift, incapable of being carried out
in life. This applies alike to the soviets as the foundation, and to the Constituent Assembly and the general
suffrage law.

[The Bolsheviks designated the soviets as reactionary because their majority consisted of peasants (peasant and soldier delegates). After the Soviets went
over to them, they became correct representatives of
popular opinion. But this sudden change was con-
nected only with the peace and land questions.] [18]

But the Constituent Assembly and the suffrage law
do not exhaust the matter. We did not consider above
the destruction of the most important democratic
guarantees of a healthy public life and of the political
activity of the laboring masses: freedom of the press,
the rights of association and assembly, which have
been outlawed for all opponents of the Soviet regime.
For these attacks (on democratic rights), the arguments of Trotsky cited above, on the cumbersome nature of democratic electoral bodies, are far from sat-
isfactory. On the other hand, it is a well-known and

---

18.   The three sentences contained within the brackets
were found as a note on an unnumbered loose sheet of
paper in the manuscript. It is probable that Rosa Luxemburg intended them as an expansion of the preceding sentence, namely: "This applies alike to the soviets as the
foundation, and to the Constituent Assembly and the general suffrage law." This sentence was crossed out in the
original manuscript, indicating that the writer intended to
rework it, or develop it further in some other form.

indisputable fact that without a free and untrammelled press, without the unlimited right of association and assemblage, the rule of the broad mass of the people is entirely unthinkable.

CHAPTER VI

THE PROBLEM OF DICTATORSHIP

LENIN says: the bourgeois state is an instrument of oppression of the working class; the socialist state, of the bourgeoisie. To a certain extent, he says, it is only the capitalist state stood on its head. This simplified view misses the most essential thing: bourgeois class rule has no need of the political training and education of the entire mass of the people, at least not beyond certain narrow limits. But for the proletarian dictatorship that is the life element, the very air without which it is not able to exist.

"Thanks to the open and direct struggle for governmental power," writes Trotsky, "the laboring masses accumulate in the shortest time a considerable amount of political experience and advance quickly from one stage to another of their development."

Here Trotsky refutes himself and his own friends. Just because this is so, they have blocked up the fountain of political experience and the source of this rising development by their suppression of public life! Or else we would have to assume that experience and development were necessary up to the seizure of power by the Bolsheviks, and then, having reached their highest peak, became superfluous thereafter. (Lenin's speech: Russia is won for socialism!!!)

In reality, the opposite is true! It is the very giant tasks which the Bolsheviks have undertaken with courage and determination that demand the most intensive political training of the masses and the accumulation of experience.

Freedom only for the supporters of the government, only for the members of one party—however numerous they may be—is no freedom at all. Freedom is always and exclusively freedom for the one who thinks differently. Not because of any fanatical concept of "justice" but because all that is instructive, wholesome and purifying in political freedom depends on this essential characteristic, and its effectiveness vanishes when "freedom" becomes a special privilege.

The Bolsheviks themselves will not want, with hand on heart, to deny that, step by step, they have to feel out the ground, try out, experiment, test now one way now another, and that a good many of their measures do not represent priceless pearls of wisdom. Thus it must and will be with all of us when we get to the same point—even if the same difficult circumstances may not prevail everywhere.

The tacit assumption underlying the Lenin-Trotsky theory of the dictatorship is this: that the socialist transformation is something for which a ready-made formula lies completed in the pocket of the revolutionary party, which needs only to be carried out energetically in practise. This is, unfortunately—or perhaps fortunately—not the case. Far from being a sum of ready-made prescriptions which have only to be applied, the practical realization of socialism as an economic, social and juridical system is something which lies completely hidden in the mists of the future. What we possess in our program is nothing but a few main signposts which indicate the general direction in which to look for the necessary measures, and the indications are mainly negative in character at that. Thus we know more or less what we must eliminate at the outset in order to free the road for a socialist economy. But when it comes to the nature of the thousand concrete, practical measures, large and small, necessary to introduce socialist principles into economy, law and all social relationships, there is no key in any socialist party program or textbook. That is not a shortcoming but rather the very thing that makes scientific socialism superior to the utopian varieties. The socialist system of society should only be, and can only be, an historical product, born out of the school of its own experiences, born in the course of its realization, as a result of the developments of living history, which—just like organic nature of which, in the last analysis, it forms a part— has the fine habit of always producing along with any real social need the means to its satisfaction, along with the task simultaneously the solution. However, if such is the case, then it is clear that socialism by its very nature cannot be decreed or introduced by *ukase*. It has as its prerequisite a number of measures of force—against property, etc. The negative, the tearing down, can be decreed; the building up, the positive, cannot. New territory. A thousand problems. Only experience is capable of correcting and opening new ways. Only unobstructed, effervescing life falls into a thousand new forms and improvisations, brings to light creative force, itself corrects all mistaken attempts. The public life of countries with limited freedom is so poverty-stricken, so miserable, so rigid, so unfruitful, precisely because, through the exclusion of democracy, it cuts off the living sources of all spiritual riches and progress. (Proof: the year 1905 and the months from February to October 1917.) There it was political in character; the same thing applies to economic and social life also. The whole mass of the people must take part in it. Otherwise, socialism will be decreed from behind a few official desks by a dozen intellectuals.

Public control is indispensably necessary. Otherwise the exchange of experiences remains only with the closed circle of the officials of the new regime. Corruption becomes inevitable. (Lenin's words, Bulletin No. 29) Socialism in life demands a complete spiritual transformation in the masses degraded by centuries of bourgeois class rule. Social instincts in place of egotistical ones, mass initiative in place of inertia, idealism which conquers all suffering, etc., etc. No one knows this better, describes it more penetratingly; repeats it more stubbornly than Lenin. But he is completely mistaken in the means he employs. Decree, dictatorial force of the factory overseer, draconic penalties, rule by terror—all these things are but palliatives. The only way to a rebirth is the school of public life itself, the most unlimited, the broadest democracy and public opinion. It is rule by terror which demoralizes.

When all this is eliminated, what really remains? In place of the representative bodies created by general, popular elections, Lenin and Trotsky have laid down the soviets as the only true representation of the laboring masses. But with the repression of political life in the land as a whole, life in the soviets must also become more and more crippled. Without general elections, without unrestricted freedom of press and assembly, without a free struggle of opinion, life dies out in every public institution, becomes a mere semblance of life, in which only the bureaucracy remains as the active element. Public life gradually falls asleep, a few dozen party leaders of inexhaustible energy and boundless experience direct and rule. Among them, in reality only a dozen outstanding heads do the leading and an elite of the working class is invited from time to time to meetings where they are to applaud the speeches of the leaders, and to approve proposed resolutions unanimously—at bottom, then, a clique affair—a dictatorship, to be sure, not the dictatorship of the proletariat, however, but only the dictatorship of a handful of politicians, that is a dictatorship in the bourgeois sense, in the sense of the rule of the Jacobins (the postponement of the Soviet Congress from three-month periods to six-month period!) Yes, we can go even further: such conditions must inevitably cause a brutalization of public life: attempted assassinations, shooting of hostages, etc. (Lenin's speech on discipline and corruption.)

CHAPTER VII

THE STRUGGLE AGAINST CORRUPTION

A PROBLEM which is of great importance in every revolution is that of the struggle with the *Lumpenproletariat*.[19] We in Germany too, as everywhere else, will have this problem to reckon with. The *Lumpenproletarian* element is deeply embedded in bourgeois society. It is not merely a special section, a sort of social wastage which grows enormously when the walls of the social order are falling down, but rather an integral part of the social whole. Events in Germany—and more or less in other countries—have shown how easily all sections of bourgeois society are subject to such degeneration. The gradations between

---

19. Roughly translatable as *slum proletariat,* the term covers the outcast, degenerated and submerged elements that make up a considerable section of the population of the great industrial centers of all modern lands. It includes beggars, prostitutes, gangsters, racketeers, swindlers, petty criminals, tramps, chronic unemployed or unemployables, persons broken in health or advanced in years who have been cast out by industry, and all sorts of declassed, degraded or degenerated elements. In times of prolonged crisis, innumerable young people also, who cannot find an opportunity to enter into the social organism as producers, may be recruited into this limbo of the outcast. Here demagogues and fascists of various stripes find some of their mass base in time of struggle and social breakdown, when the ranks of the *Lumpenproletariat* are enormously swelled by ruined and declassed elements from all layers of a disintegrating society.

commercial profiteering, fictitious deals, adulteration of foodstuffs, cheating, official embezzlement, theft, burglary and robbery, flow into one another in such fashion that the boundary line between honorable citizenry and the penitentiary has disappeared. In this the same phenomenon is repeated as in the regular and rapid degeneration of bourgeois dignitaries when they are transplanted to an alien social soil in an overseas colonial setting. With the stripping off of conventional barriers and props for morality and law, bourgeois society itself falls victim to direct and limitless degeneration (*Verlumpung*), for its innermost law of life is the profoundest of immoralities, namely, the exploitation of man by man. The proletarian revolution will have to struggle with this enemy and instrument of counter-revolution on every hand.

And yet, in this connection too, terror is a dull, nay, a two-edged sword. The harshest measures of martial law are impotent against outbreaks of the *lumpenproletarian* sickness. Indeed, every persistent regime of martial law leads inevitably to arbitrariness, and every form of arbitrariness tends to deprave society. In this regard also, the only effective means in the hands of the proletarian revolution are: radical measures of a political and social character, the speediest possible transformation of the social guarantees of the life of the masses—the kindling of revolutionary idealism, which can be maintained over any length of time only through the intensively active life of the masses themselves under conditions of unlimited political freedom.

As the free action of the sun's rays is the most effective purifying and healing remedy against infections and disease germs, so the only healing and purifying sun is the revolution itself and its renovating principle, the spiritual life, activity and initiative of the masses which is called into being by it and which takes the form of the broadest political freedom.[20]

In our case as everywhere else, anarchy will be unavoidable. The *lumpenproletarian* element is deeply embedded in bourgeois society and inseparable from it.

Proofs:

1. East Prussia, the "Cossack" robberies.

2. The general outbreak of robbery and theft in Germany. (Profiteering, postal and railway personnel, police, complete dissolution of the boundaries between well-ordered society and the penitentiary.)

3. The rapid degeneration (*Verlumpung*) of the union leaders.

Against this, draconian measures of terror are powerless. On the contrary, they cause still further corruption. The only anti-toxin: the idealism and social activity of the masses, unlimited political freedom.

That is an overpowering objective law from which no party can be exempt.

---

20. The above passages on the *Lumpenproletariat* are apparently an elaboration of the following paragraphs which repeat substantially the same ideas in more schematic form and were found in the original manuscript on a separate sheet of paper.

CHAPTER VIII

DEMOCRACY AND DICTATORSHIP

THE basic error of the Lenin-Trotsky theory is that they too, just like Kautsky, oppose dictatorship to democracy. "Dictatorship *or* democracy" is the way the question is put by Bolsheviks and Kautsky alike. The latter naturally decides in favor of "democracy," that is, of bourgeois democracy, precisely because he opposes it to the alternative of the socialist revolution. Lenin and Trotsky, on the other hand, decide in favor of dictatorship in contradistinction to democracy, and thereby, in favor of the dictatorship of a handful of persons, that is, in favor of dictatorship on the bourgeois model. They are two opposite poles, both alike being far removed from a genuine socialist policy. The proletariat, when it seizes power, can never follow the good advice of Kautsky, given on the pretext of the "unripeness of the country," the advice being to renounce the socialist revolution and devote itself to democracy. It cannot follow this advice without betraying thereby itself, the International, and the revolution. It should and must at once undertake socialist measures in the most energetic, unyielding and unhesitant fashion, in other words, exercise a dictatorship, but a dictatorship of the *class*, not of a party or of a clique—dictatorship of the class, that means in the broadest public form on the basis of the most active, unlimited participation of the mass of the people, of unlimited democracy.

"As Marxists," writes Trotsky, "we have never been idol worshippers of formal democracy." Surely, we have never been idol worshippers of formal democracy. Nor have we ever been idol worshippers of socialism or Marxism either. Does it follow from this that we may also throw socialism on the scrap-heap, a la Cunow, Lensch and Parvus, if it becomes uncomfortable for us? Trotsky and Lenin are the living refutation of this answer.

"We have never been idol-worshippers of formal democracy." All that that really means is: We have always distinguished the social kernel from the political form of *bourgeois* democracy; we have always revealed the hard kernel of social inequality and lack of freedom hidden under the sweet shell of formal equality and freedom—not in order to reject the latter but to spur the working class into not being satisfied with the shell, but rather, by conquering political power, to create a socialist democracy to re place bourgeois democracy—not to eliminate democ racy altogether.

But socialist democracy is not something which begins only in the promised land after the foundations of socialist economy are created; it does not come as some sort of Christmas present for the worthy people who, in the interim, have loyally supported a handful of socialist dictators. Socialist democracy begins simultaneously with the beginnings of the destruction of class rule and of the construction of socialism. It begins at the very moment of the seizure of power by the socialist party. It is the same thing as the dictatorship of the proletariat.

Yes, dictatorship! But this dictatorship consists in

the *manner of applying democracy,* not in its *elimination,* in energetic, resolute attacks upon the well-
entrenched rights and economic relationships of bourgeois society, without which a socialist transformation cannot be accomplished. But this dictatorship
must be the work of the *class* and not of a little leading minority in the name of the class—that is, it must
proceed step by step out of the active participation
of the masses; it must be under their direct influence,
subjected to the control of complete public activity;
it must arise out of the growing political training of
the mass of the people.

Doubtless the Bolsheviks would have proceeded in
this very way were it not that they suffered under
the frightful compulsion of the world war, the German occupation and all the abnormal difficulties con-
nected therewith, things which were inevitably bound
to distort any socialist policy, however imbued it
might be with the best intentions and the finest principles.

A crude proof of this is provided by the use of
terror to so wide an extent by the Soviet government,
especially in the most recent period just before the
collapse of German imperialism, and just after the
attempt on the life of the German ambassador. The
commonplace to the effect that revolutions are not
pink teas is in itself pretty inadequate.

Everything that happens in Russia is comprehen-
sible and represents an inevitable chain of causes and
effects, the starting point and end term of which are:
the failure of the German proletariat and the occupation of Russia by German imperialism. It would be
demanding something superhuman from Lenin and
his comrades if we should expect of them that under
such circumstances they should conjure forth the

finest democracy, the most exemplary dictatorship of the proletariat and a flourishing socialist economy. By their determined revolutionary stand, their exemplary strength in action, and their unbreakable loyalty to international socialism, they have contributed whatever could possibly be contributed under such devilishly hard conditions. The danger begins only when they make a virtue of necessity and want to freeze into a complete theoretical system all the tactics forced upon them by these fatal circumstances, and want to recommend them to the international proletariat as a model of socialist tactics. When they get in their own light in this way, and hide their genuine, unquestionable historical service under the bushel of false steps forced upon them by necessity, they render a poor service to international socialism for the sake of which they have fought and suffered; for they want to place in its storehouse as new discoveries all the distortions prescribed in Russia by necessity and compulsion—in the last analysis only by-products of the bankruptcy of international socialism in the present world war.

Let the German Government Socialists cry that the rule of the Bolsheviks in Russia is a distorted expression of the dictatorship of the proletariat. If it was or is such, that is only because it is a product of the behavior of the German proletariat, in itself a distorted expression of the socialist class struggle. All of us are subject to the laws of history, and it is only internationally that the socialist order of society can be realized. The Bolsheviks have shown that they are capable of everything that a genuine revolutionary party can contribute within the limits of the historical possibilities. They are not supposed to perform miracles. For a model and faultless proletarian revolution in an isolated land, exhausted by world war, strangled by imperialism, betrayed by the international proletariat, would be a miracle.

What is in order is to distinguish the essential from the non-essential, the kernel from the accidental excrescences in the policies of the Bolsheviks. In the present period, when we face decisive final struggles in all the world, the most important problem of socialism was and is the burning question of our time. It is not a matter of this or that secondary question of tactics, but of the capacity for action of the proletariat, the strength to act, the will to power of socialism as such. In this, Lenin and Trotsky and their friends were the *first,* those who went ahead as an example to the proletariat of the world; they are still the *only ones* up to now who can cry with Hutten: "I have dared!"

This is the essential and *enduring* in Bolshevik policy. In *this* sense theirs is the immortal historical service of having marched at the head of the international proletariat with the conquest of political power and the practical placing of the problem of the realization of socialism, and of having advanced mightily the settlement of the score between capital and labor in the entire world. In Russia the problem could only be posed. It could not be solved in Russia. And in *this* sense, the future everywhere belongs to "Bolshevism."

LENINISM OR MARXISM?

This article first appeared in *Iskra,* the theoretic organ of the Russian Social Democratic Party and in the German *Neue Zeit,* in 1904, under the original title of "Organizational Questions of the Russian Social Democracy." It appeared also in pamphlet form under the title *Marxism vs. Leninism.*

I

An unprecedented task in the history of the socialist movement has fallen to the lot of the Russian Social Democracy. It is the task of deciding on what is the best socialist tactical policy in a country where absolute monarchy is still dominant. It is a mistake to draw a rigid parallel between the present Russian situation and that which existed in Germany during the years 1878–90, when Bismarck's antisocialist laws were in force. The two have one thing in common—police rule. Otherwise, they are in no way comparable.

The obstacles offered to the socialist movement by the absence of democratic liberties are of relatively secondary importance. Even in Russia, the people's movement has succeeded in overcoming the barriers set up by the state. The people have found themselves a "constitution" (though a rather precarious one) in street disorders. Persevering in this course, the Russian people will in time attain complete victory over the autocracy.

The principal difficulty faced by socialist activity in Russia results from the fact that in that country the domination of the bourgeoisie is veiled by absolutist force. This gives socialist propaganda an abstract character, while immediate political agitation takes on a democratic-revolutionary guise.

Bismarck's antisocialist laws put our movement out of constitutional bounds in a highly developed bourgeois society, where class antagonisms had already reached their full bloom in parliamentary contests. (Here, by the way, lay the absurdity of Bismarck's scheme.) The situation is quite different in Russia. The problem there is how to create a Social Democratic movement at a time when the state is not yet in the hands of the bourgeoisie.

This circumstance has an influence on agitation, on the manner of transplanting socialist doctrine to Russian soil. It also bears in a peculiar and direct way on the question of *party organization*.

Under ordinary conditions—that is, where the political domination of the bourgeoisie has preceded the socialist movement—the bourgeoisie itself instills in the working class the rudiments of political solidarity. At this stage, declares the Communist Manifesto, the unification of the workers is not yet the result of their own aspiration to unity but comes as a result of the activity of the bourgeoisie, "which, in order to attain its own political ends, is compelled to set the proletariat in motion . . ."

In Russia, however, the Social Democracy must make up by its own efforts an entire historic period. It must lead the Russian proletarians from their present "atomized" condition, which prolongs the autocratic regime, to a class organization that would help them to become aware of their historic objectives and prepare them to struggle to achieve those objectives.

The Russian socialists are obliged to undertake the building of such an organization without the benefit of the formal guarantees commonly found under a bourgeois-democratic setup. They do not dispose of the political raw material that in other countries is supplied by bourgeois society itself. Like God Almighty they must have this organization arise out of the void, so to speak.

How to effect a transition from the type of organization characteristic of the preparatory stage of the socialist movement—usually featured by disconnected local groups and clubs, with propaganda as a principal activity—to the unity of a large, national body, suitable for concerted political action over the entire vast territory ruled by the Russian state? That is the specific problem which the Russian Social Democracy has mulled over for some time.

Autonomy and isolation are the most pronounced characteristics of the old organizational type. It is, therefore, understandable why the slogan of the persons who want to see an inclusive national organization should be "Centralism!"

Centralism was the theme of the campaign that has been carried on by the *Iskra* group for the last three years. This campaign has produced the Congress of August 1903, which has been described as the second congress of the Russian Social Democratic Party but was, in fact, its constituent assembly.

At the Party Congress, it became evident that the term "centralism" does not completely cover the question of organization for the Russian Social Democracy. Once again we have learned that no rigid formula can furnish the solution of any problem in the socialist movement.

One Step Forward, Two Steps Backward, written by Lenin, an outstanding member of the *Iskra* group, is a methodical exposition of the ideas of the ultra-centralist tendency in the Russian movement. The viewpoint presented with incomparable vigor and logic in this book, is that of pitiless centralism. Laid down as principles are: 1. The necessity of selecting, and constituting as a separate corps, all the active revolutionists, as distinguished from the unorganized, though revolutionary, mass surrounding this elite.

N.B.

Lenin's thesis is that the party Central Committee should have the privilege of naming all the local committees of the party. It should have the right to appoint the effective organs of all local bodies from Geneva to Liège, from Tomsk to Irkutsk.[1] It should also have the right to impose on all of them its own ready-made rules of party conduct. It should have the right to rule without appeal on such questions

---

1 Many Russian socialists carried on their revolutionary activities from places in Western Europe, while thousands lived as deportees in Siberia and Central Asia. The tsarist state was an inefficient and easygoing authoritarian machine, much inferior in its methods of repression to the modern Soviet state. The Siberian exiles were allowed a great deal of freedom of action, which did not even exclude political activity on the part of the deportees. The tsarist state did not apply scientific know-how to the business of repression. It is interesting to note that the concentration camp of our epoch first appears in politics as the post-revolutionary, Bolshevik "isolator." It can be said that the intimation of this scientific political appliance can be located in the proposals of the "outstanding member of the *Iskra* group" discussed by Rosa Luxemburg in this learned essay.—Translator.

as the dissolution and reconstitution of local organizations. This way, the Central Committee could
determine, to suit itself, the composition of the highest party organs as well as of the party congress. The
Central Committee would be the only thinking element in the party. All other groupings would be its
executive limbs.

Lenin reasons that the combination of the socialist mass movement with such a rigorously centralized type of organization is a specific principle of
revolutionary Marxism. To support this thesis, he
advances a series of arguments, with which we shall
deal below.

Generally speaking it is undeniable that a strong
tendency toward centralization is inherent in the
Social Democratic movement. This tendency springs
from the economic makeup of capitalism which is
essentially a centralizing factor. The Social Democratic movement carries on its activity inside the
large bourgeois city. Its mission is to represent,
within the boundaries of the national state, the class
interests of the proletariat, and to oppose those
common interests to all local and group interests.

Therefore, the Social Democracy is, as a rule, hos-
tile to any manifestations of localism or federalism.
It strives to unite all workers and all worker organizations in a single party, no matter what national,
religious, or occupational differences may exist
among them. The Social Democracy abandons this
principle and gives way to federalism only under
exceptional conditions, as in the case of the Austro-
Hungarian Empire.

It is clear that the Russian Social Democracy
should not organize itself as a federative conglomer-
ate of many national groups. It must rather become

a single party for the entire empire. However, that
is not really the question considered here. What
we are considering is the degree of centralization
necessary inside the unified, single Russian party
in view of the peculiar conditions under which it
has to function.

Looking at the matter from the angle of the formal tasks of the Social Democracy in its capacity as
a party of class struggle, it appears at first that the
power and energy of the party are directly depend-
ent on the possibility of centralizing the party.
However, these formal tasks apply to all active parties. In the case of the Social Democracy, they are
less important than is the influence of historic conditions.

N.B. The Social Democratic movement is the first in
the history of class societies which reckons, in all
its phases and through its entire course, on the organization and the direct, independent action of the
masses.

Because of this, the Social Democracy creates an
organizational type that is entirely different from
those common to earlier revolutionary movements,
such as those of the Jacobins and the adherents of
Blanqui.

Lenin seems to slight this fact when he presents
in his book (page 140) the opinion that the revolutionary Social Democrat is nothing else than a
"Jacobin indissolubly joined to the organization of
the proletariat, which has become conscious of its
class interests."

For Lenin, the difference between the Social
Democracy and Blanquism is reduced to the obser-
vation that in place of a handful of conspirators we
have a class-conscious proletariat. He forgets that

this difference implies a complete revision of our ideas on organization and, therefore, an entirely different conception of centralism and the relations existing between the party and the struggle itself.

Blanquism did not count on the direct action of the working class. It, therefore, did not need to organize the people for the revolution. The people were expected to play their part only at the moment of revolution. Preparation for the revolution concerned only the little group of revolutionists armed for the coup. Indeed, to assure the success of the revolutionary conspiracy, it was considered wiser to keep the mass at some distance from the conspirators. Such a relationship could be conceived by the Blanquists only because there was no close contact between the conspiratorial activity of their organization and the daily struggle of the popular masses.

The tactics and concrete tasks of the Blanquist revolutionists had little connection with the elementary class struggle. They were freely improvised. They could, therefore, be decided on in advance and took the form of a ready-made plan. In consequence of this, ordinary members of the organization became simple executive organs, carrying out the orders of a will fixed beforehand, and outside of their particular sphere of activity. They became the instruments of a Central Committee. Here we have the second peculiarity of conspiratorial centralism—the absolute and blind submission of the party sections to the will of the center, and the extension of this authority to all parts of the organization.

However, Social Democratic activity is carried on under radically different conditions. It arises historically out of the elementary class struggle. It spreads and develops in accordance with the following dia-

lectical contradiction. The proletarian army is recruited and becomes aware of its objectives in the
course of the struggle itself. The activity of the party
organization, the growth of the proletarians' awareness of the objectives of the struggle and the struggle
itself, are not different things separated chronologi-
cally and mechanically. They are only different aspects of the same process. Except for the general
principles of the struggle, there do not exist for the
Social Democracy detailed sets of tactics which a
Central Committee can teach the party membership
in the same way as troops are instructed in their
training camps. Furthermore, the range of influence
of the socialist party is constantly fluctuating with
the ups and downs of the struggle in the course of
which the organization is created and grows.

For this reason Social Democratic centralism cannot be based on the mechanical subordination and
blind obedience of the party membership to the
leading party center. For this reason, the Social
Democratic movement cannot allow the erection of
an air-tight partition between the class-conscious nucleus of the proletariat already in the party and its
immediate popular environment, the nonparty sections of the proletariat.

Now the two principles on which Lenin's centralism rests are precisely these: 1. The blind subordination, in the smallest detail, of all party organs,
to the party center, which alone thinks, guides, and
decides for all. 2. The rigorous separation of the organized nucleus of revolutionaries from its social-
revolutionary surroundings.

Such centralism is a mechanical transposition of
the organizational principles of Blanquism into the
mass movement of the socialist working class.

In accordance with this view, Lenin defines his "revolutionary Social Democrat" as a "Jacobin joined to the organization of the proletariat, which has become conscious of its class interests."

The fact is that the Social Democracy is not *joined* to the organization of the proletariat. It is itself the proletariat. And because of this, Social Democratic centralism is essentially different from Blanquist centralism. It can only be the concentrated will of the individuals and groups representative of the most class-conscious, militant, advanced sections of the working class. It is, so to speak, the "self-centralism" of the advanced sectors of the proletariat. It is the rule of the majority within its own party.

The indispensable conditions for the realization of Social-Democratic centralism are: 1. The existence of a large contingent of workers educated in the political struggle. 2. The possibility for the workers to develop their own political activity through direct influence on public life, in a party press, and public congresses, etc.

These conditions are not yet fully formed in Russia. The first—a proletarian vanguard, conscious of its class interests and capable of self-direction in political activity—is only now emerging in Russia. All efforts of socialist agitation and organization should aim to hasten the formation of such a vanguard. The second condition can be had only under a regime of political liberty.

With these conclusions, Lenin disagrees violently. He is convinced that all the conditions necessary for the formation of a powerful and centralized party already exist in Russia. He declares that "it is no longer the proletarians but certain intellectuals in our party who need to be educated in the matters of organization and discipline" (page 145). He glorifies the educative influence of the factory, which, he says, accustoms the proletariat to "discipline and organization" (page 147).

Saying all this, Lenin seems to demonstrate again that his conception of socialist organization is quite mechanistic. The discipline Lenin has in mind is being implanted in the working class not only by the factory but also by the military and the existing state bureaucracy—by the entire mechanism of the centralized bourgeois state.

We misuse words and we practice self-deception when we apply the same term—discipline—to such dissimilar notions as: 1, the absence of thought and will in a body with a thousand automatically moving hands and legs, and 2, the spontaneous co-ordination of the conscious, political acts of a body of men. What is there in common between the regulated docility of an oppressed class and the self-discipline and organization of a class struggling for its emancipation?

The self-discipline of the Social Democracy is not merely the replacement of the authority of the bourgeois rulers with the authority of a socialist central committee. The working class will acquire the sense of the new discipline, the freely assumed self-discipline of the Social Democracy, not as a result of the discipline imposed on it by the capitalist state, but by extirpating, to the last root, its old habits of obedience and servility.

Centralism in the socialist sense is not an absolute thing applicable to any phase whatsoever of the labor movement. It is a *tendency*, which becomes real in proportion to the development and political training acquired by the working masses in the course of their struggle.

No doubt, the absence of the conditions necessary
for the complete realization of this kind of centralism in the Russian movement presents a formidable
obstacle.

It is a mistake to believe that it is possible to sub-
stitute "provisionally" the absolute power of a
Central Committee (acting somehow by "tacit delegation") for the yet unrealizable rule of the majority
of conscious workers in the party, and in this way re-
place the open control of the working masses over
the party organs with the reverse control by the
Central Committee over the revolutionary proletariat.

The history of the Russian labor movement suggests the doubtful value of such centralism. An all-
powerful center, invested, as Lenin would have it,
with the unlimited right to control and intervene,
would be an absurdity if its authority applied only
to technical questions, such as the administration
of funds, the distribution of tasks among propagan-
dists and agitators, the transportation and circula-
tion of printed matter. The political purpose of an
organ having such great powers is understandable
only if those powers apply to the elaboration of a
uniform plan of action, if the central organ assumes
the initiative of a vast revolutionary act.

But what has been the experience of the Russian
socialist movement up to now? The most important
and most fruitful changes in its tactical policy during the last ten years have not been the inventions
of several leaders and even less so of any central
organizational organs. They have always been the
spontaneous product of the movement in ferment.
This was true during the first stage of the proletarian movement in Russia, which began with the

spontaneous general strike of St. Petersburg in 1896,
an event that marks the inception of an epoch of
economic struggle by the Russian working people.
It was no less true during the following period, introduced by the spontaneous street demonstrations
of St. Petersburg students in March 1901. The general strike of Rostov-on-Don, in 1903, marking the
next great tactical turn in the Russian proletarian
movement, was also a spontaneous act. "All by itself," the strike expanded into political demonstrations, street agitation, great outdoor meetings,
which the most optimistic revolutionist would not
have dreamed of several years before.

Our cause made great gains in these events. However, the initiative and conscious leadership of the
Social Democratic organizations played an insignificant role in this development. It is true that these
organizations were not specifically prepared for such
happenings. However, the unimportant part played
by the revolutionists cannot be explained by this
fact. Neither can it be attributed to the absence of
an all-powerful central party apparatus similar to
what is asked for by Lenin. The existence of such a
guiding center would have probably increased the
disorder of the local committees by emphasizing
the difference between the eager attack of the mass
and the prudent position of the Social Democracy.
The same phenomenon—the insignificant part
played by the initiative of central party organs in
the elaboration of actual tactical policy—can be observed today in Germany and other countries. In
general, the tactical policy of the Social Democracy
is not something that may be "invented." It is the
product of a series of great creative acts of the often
spontaneous class struggle seeking its way forward.

The unconscious comes before the conscious. The logic of the historic process comes before the sub-   N.B. jective logic of the human beings who participate in the historic process. The tendency is for the directing organs of the socialist party to play a conservative role. Experience shows that every time the labor movement wins new terrain those organs work it to the utmost. They transform it at the same time into a kind of bastion, which holds up advance on a wider scale.

The present tactical policy of the German Social Democracy has won universal esteem because it is supple as well as firm. This is a sign of the fine adaptation of the party, in the smallest detail of its everyday activity, to the conditions of a parliamentary regime. The party has made a methodical study of all the resources of this terrain. It knows how to utilize them without modifying its principles.

However, the very perfection of this adaptation is already closing vaster horizons to our party. There is a tendency in the party to regard parliamentary tactics as the immutable and specific tactics of socialist activity. People refuse, for example, to consider the possibility (posed by Parvus) of changing our tactical policy in case general suffrage is abolished in Germany, an eventuality not considered entirely improbable by the leaders of the German Social Democracy.

Such inertia is due, in a large degree, to the fact that it is very inconvenient to define, within the vacuum of abstract hypotheses, the lines and forms of still nonexistent political situations. Evidently, the important thing for the Social Democracy is not the preparation of a set of directives all ready for future policy. It is important: 1, to encourage a correct historic appreciation of the forms of struggle corresponding to the given situations, and 2, to maintain an understanding of the relativity of the current phase and the inevitable increase of revolutionary tension as the final goal of the class struggle is approached.

Granting, as Lenin wants, such absolute powers of a negative character to the top organ of the party, we strengthen, to a dangerous extent, the conservatism inherent in such an organ. If the tactics of the socialist party are not to be the creation of a Central Committee but of the whole party, or, still better, of the whole labor movement, then it is clear that the party sections and federations need the liberty of action which alone will permit them to develop their revolutionary initiative and to utilize all the resources of a situation. The ultra-centralism asked by Lenin is full of the sterile spirit of the overseer. It is not a positive and creative spirit. *Lenin's concern is not so much to make the activity of the party more fruitful as to control the party—to narrow the movement rather than to develop it, to bind rather than to unify it.*

N.B.

In the present situation, such an experiment would be doubly dangerous to the Russian Social Democracy. It stands on the eve of decisive battles against tsarism. It is about to enter, or has already entered, on a period of intensified creative activity, during which it will broaden (as is usual in a revolutionary period) its sphere of influence and will advance spontaneously by leaps and bounds. To attempt to bind the initiative of the party at this moment, to surround it with a network of barbed wire, is to render it incapable of accomplishing the tremendous tasks of the hour.

N.B.

The general ideas we have presented on the question of socialist centralism are not by themselves sufficient for the formulation of a constitutional plan suiting the Russian party. In the final instance, a statute of this kind can only be determined by the conditions under which the activity of the organization takes place in a given epoch. The question of the moment in Russia is how to set in motion a large proletarian organization. No constitutional project can claim infallibility. It must prove itself in fire.

But from our general conception of the nature of Social Democratic organization, we feel justified in deducing that its spirit requires—especially at the inception of the mass party—the co-ordination and unification of the movement and not its rigid submission to a set of regulations. If the party possesses the gift of political mobility, complemented by unflinching loyalty to principles and concern for unity, we can rest assured that any defects in the party constitution will be corrected in practice. For us, it is not the letter, but the living spirit carried into the organization by the membership that decides the value of this or that organizational form.   N.B.

II

So far we have examined the problem of centralism from the viewpoint of the general principles of the Social Democracy, and to some extent, in the light of conditions peculiar to Russia. However, the military ultra-centralism cried up by Lenin and his friends is not the product of accidental differences of opinion. It is said to be related to a campaign against opportunism which Lenin has carried to the smallest organizational detail.

"It is important," says Lenin (page 52), "to forge a more or less effective weapon against opportunism." He believes that opportunism springs specifically from the characteristic leaning of intellectuals to decentralization and disorganization, from their aversion for strict discipline and "bureaucracy," which is, however, necessary for the functioning of the party.

Lenin says that intellectuals remain individualists and tend to anarchism even after they have joined the socialist movement. According to him, it is only among intellectuals that we can note a repugnance for the absolute authority of a Central Committee. The authentic proletarian, Lenin suggests, finds by reason of his class instinct a kind of voluptuous pleasure in abandoning himself to the clutch of firm leadership and pitiless discipline. "To oppose bureaucracy to democracy," writes Lenin, "is to contrast the organizational principle of revolutionary Social Democracy to the methods of opportunist organization" (page 151).

He declares that a similar conflict between centralizing and autonomist tendencies is taking place in all countries where reformism and revolutionary socialism meet face to face. He points in particular to the recent controversy in the German Social Democracy on the question of the degree of freedom of action to be allowed by the Party to socialist representatives in legislative assemblies.

Let us examine the parallels drawn by Lenin.

First, it is important to point out that the glorification of the supposed genius of proletarians in the matter of socialist organization and a general distrust of intellectuals as such are not necessarily signs of "revolutionary Marxist" mentality. It is very easy to demonstrate that such arguments are themselves an expression of opportunism.

Antagonism between purely proletarian elements and the nonproletarian intellectuals in the labor movement is raised as an ideological issue by the following trends: the semianarchism of the French syndicalists, whose watchword is "Beware of the politician!"; English trade-unionism, full of mistrust of the "socialist visionaries"; and, if our information is correct, the "pure economism," represented a short while ago within the Russian Social Democracy by *Rabochaya Mysl* ("Labor Thought"), which was printed secretly in St. Petersburg.

In most socialist parties of Western Europe there is undoubtedly a connection between opportunism and the "intellectuals," as well as between opportunism and decentralizing tendencies within the labor movement.

But nothing is more contrary to the historic-dialectic method of Marxist thought than to separate social phenomena from their historic soil and to present these phenomena as abstract formulas having an absolute, general application. N.B.

Reasoning abstractly, we may say that the "intellectual," a social element which has emerged out of the bourgeoisie and is therefore alien to the proletariat, enters the socialist movement not because of his natural class inclinations but in spite of them. For this reason, he is more liable to opportunist aberrations than the proletarian. The latter, we say, can be expected to find a definite revolutionary point of support in his class interests as long as he does not leave his original environment, the laboring mass. But the concrete form assumed by this inclination of the intellectual toward opportunism and, above all, the manner in which this tendency expresses itself in organizational questions depend every time on his given social milieu.

Bourgeois parliamentarism is the definite social base of the phenomena observed by Lenin in the German, French, and Italian socialist movements. This parliamentarism is the breeding place of all the opportunist tendencies now existing in the Western Social Democracy.

The kind of parliamentarism we now have in France, Italy, and Germany provides the soil for such illusions of current opportunism as overvaluation of social reforms, class and party collaboration, the hope of pacific development toward socialism, etc. It does so by placing intellectuals, acting in the capacity of parliamentarians, above the proletariat and by separating intellectuals from proletarians inside the socialist party itself. With the growth of the labor movement, parliamentarism becomes a springboard for political careerists. That is why so many ambitious failures from the bourgeoisie flock to the banners of the socialist parties. Another source of contemporary opportunism is the considerable material means and influence of the large Social Democratic organizations.

The party acts as a bulwark protecting the class movement against digressions in the direction of more bourgeois parliamentarism. To triumph, these tendencies must destroy the bulwark. They must dissolve the active, class-conscious sector of the proletariat in the amorphous mass of an "electorate."

That is how the "autonomist" and decentralizing tendencies arise in our Social Democratic parties. We notice that these tendencies suit definite political ends. They cannot be explained, as Lenin attempts, by referring to the intellectual's psychology, to his supposedly innate instability of character. They can only be explained by considering the needs of the bourgeois parliamentary politician, that is, by opportunist politics.

The situation is quite different in tsarist Russia. Opportunism in the Russian labor movement is, generally speaking, not the by-product of Social Democratic strength or of the decomposition of the bourgeoisie. It is the product of the backward political condition of Russian society.

N.B.

The milieu where intellectuals are recruited for socialism in Russia is much more declassed and by far less bourgeois than in Western Europe. Added to the immaturity of the Russian proletarian movement, this circumstance is an influence for wide theoretic wandering, which ranges from the complete negation of the political aspect of the labor movement to the unqualified belief in the effectiveness of isolated terrorist acts, or even total political indifference sought in the swamps of liberalism and Kantian idealism.

However, the intellectual within the Russian Social Democratic movement can only with difficulty be attracted to any act of disorganization. It is contrary to the general outlook of the Russian intellectual's milieu. There is no bourgeois parliament in Russia to favor this tendency.

The Western intellectual who professes at this moment the "cult of the ego" and colors even his socialist yearnings with an aristocratic morale, is not the representative of the bourgeois intelligentsia "in general." He represents only a certain phase of social development. He is the product of bourgeois decadence.

N.B.

On the other hand, the utopian or opportunist dreams of the Russian intellectual who has joined the socialist movement tend to nourish themselves on theoretic formulae in which the "ego" is not exalted but humiliated, in which the morality of renunciation, expiation, is the dominant principle.

The *Narodniki* ("Populists") of 1875 called on the Russian intelligentsia to lose themselves in the peasant mass. The ultra-civilized followers of Tolstoi speak today of escape to the life of the "simple folk." Similarly, the partisans of "pure economism" in the Russian Social Democracy want us to bow down before the "calloused hand" of labor.

If instead of mechanically applying to Russia formulae elaborated in Western Europe, we approach the problem of organization from the angle of conditions specific to Russia, we arrive at conclusions that are diametrically opposed to Lenin's.

To attribute to opportunism an invariable preference for a definite form of organization, that is, decentralization, is to miss the essence of opportunism.

On the question of organization, or any other question, opportunism knows only one principle: the absence of principle. Opportunism chooses its means of action with the aim of suiting the given circumstances at hand, provided these means appear to lead toward the ends in view.

If, like Lenin, we define opportunism as the tendency that paralyzes the independent revolutionary movement of the working class and transforms it into an instrument of ambitious bourgeois intellectuals, we must also recognize that in the initial stage of a labor movement this end is more easily attained as a result of rigorous centralization rather than by decentralization. It is by extreme centralization that a young, uneducated proletarian movement can be most completely handed over to the intellectual leaders staffing a Central Committee.

Also in Germany, at the start of the Social Democratic movement, and before the emergence of a solid nucleus of conscious proletarians and a tactical policy based on experience, partisans of the two opposite types of organization faced each other in argument. The "General Association of German Workers," founded by Lassalle, stood for extreme centralization. [*Allgemeine Deutsche Arbeiterverein,* organized on May 23, 1863.—Translator.] The principle of autonomism was supported by the party which was organized at the Eisenach Congress with the collaboration of W. Liebknecht and A. Bebel. [*Deutsche Sozialdemokratische Arbeiter Partei,* organized at Eisenach, Germany, in 1869.—Translator.]

The tactical policy of the "Eisenachers" was quite confused. Yet they contributed vastly more to the awakening of class-consciousness of the German masses than the Lassalleans. Very early the workers played a preponderant role in that party (as was demonstrated by the number of worker publications in the provinces), and there was a rapid extension of the range of the movement. At the same time, the Lassalleans, in spite of all their experiments with "dictators," led their faithful from one misadventure to another.

In general, it is rigorous, despotic centralism that is preferred by opportunist intellectuals at a time when the revolutionary elements among the workers still lack cohesion and the movement is groping its way, as is the case now in Russia. In a later phase, under a parliamentary regime and in connection

with a strong labor party, the opportunist tendencies of the intellectuals express themselves in an inclination toward "decentralization."

If we assume the viewpoint claimed as his own by
Lenin and we fear the influence of intellectuals in
the proletarian movement, we can conceive of no
greater danger to the Russian party than Lenin's
plan of organization. *Nothing will more surely en-*
slave a young labor movement to an intellectual
elite hungry for power than this bureaucratic strait
jacket, which will immobilize the movement and
turn it into an automaton manipulated by a Cen-
tral Committee. On the other hand, there is no
more effective guarantee against opportunist in-
trigue and personal ambition than the independent
revolutionary action of the proletariat, as a result
of which the workers acquire the sense of political
responsibility and self-reliance.

What is today only a phantom haunting Lenin's
imagination may become reality tomorrow.

Let us not forget that the revolution soon to break
out in Russia will be a bourgeois and not a proletarian revolution. This modifies radically all the
conditions of socialist struggle. The Russian intellectuals, too, will rapidly become imbued with
bourgeois ideology. The Social Democracy is at
present the only guide of the Russian proletariat.
But on the day after the revolution, we shall see
the bourgeoisie, and above all the bourgeois intellectuals, seek to use the masses as a steppingstone
to their domination.

The game of the bourgeois demagogues will be
made easier if at the present stage, the spontaneous
action, initiative, and political sense of the advanced
sections of the working class are hindered in their

development and restricted by the protectorate of an authoritarian Central Committee.

More important is the fundamental falseness of the idea underlying the plan of unqualified centralism—the idea that the road to opportunism can be N.B. barred by means of clauses in a party constitution.

Impressed by recent happenings in the socialist parties of France, Italy, and Germany, the Russian Social Democrats tend to regard opportunism as an alien ingredient, brought into the labor movement by representatives of bourgeois democracy. If that were so, no penalties provided by a party constitution could stop this intrusion. The afflux of nonproletarian recruits to the party of the proletariat is the effect of profound social causes, such as the economic collapse of the petty bourgeoisie, the bankruptcy of bourgeois liberalism, and the degeneration of bourgeois democracy. It is naïve to hope to stop this current by means of a formula written down in a constitution.

A manual of regulations may master the life of a small sect or a private circle. An historic current, however, will pass through the mesh of the most subtly worded statutory paragraph. It is furthermore untrue that to repel the elements pushed toward the socialist movement by the decomposition of bourgeois society means to defend the interests of the working class. The Social Democracy has always contended that it represents not only the class interests of the proletariat but also the progressive aspirations of the whole of contemporary society. It N.B. represents the interests of all who are oppressed by bourgeois domination. This must not be understood merely in the sense that all these interests are ideally contained in the socialist program. Historic evolution translates the given proposition into reality. In its capacity as a political party, the Social Democracy becomes the haven of all discontented elements in our society and thus of the entire people, as contrasted to the tiny minority of the capitalist masters.

But socialists must always know how to subordinate the anguish, rancor, and hope of this motley aggregation to the supreme goal of the working class. The Social Democracy must enclose the tumult of the nonproletarian protestants against existing society within the bounds of the revolutionary action of the proletariat. It must assimilate the elements that come to it.

This is only possible if the Social Democracy already contains a strong, politically educated proletarian nucleus class conscious enough to be able, as up to now in Germany, to pull along in its tow the declassed and petty bourgeois elements that join the party. In that case, greater strictness in the application of the principle of centralization and more severe discipline, specifically formulated in party bylaws, may be an effective safeguard against the opportunist danger. That is how the revolutionary socialist movement in France defended itself against the Jaurèsist confusion. A modification of the constitution of the German Social Democracy in that direction would be a very timely measure.

But even here we should not think of the party constitution as a weapon that is, somehow, self-sufficient. It can be at most a coercive instrument enforcing the will of the proletarian majority in the party. If this majority is lacking, then the most dire sanctions on paper will be of no avail.

However, the influx of bourgeois elements into the party is far from being the only cause of the opportunist trends that are now raising their heads in the Social Democracy. Another cause is the very nature of socialist activity and the contradictions inherent in it.

The international movement of the proletariat toward its complete emancipation is a process peculiar in the following respect. For the first time in the history of civilization, the people are expressing their will consciously and in opposition to all ruling classes. But this will can only be satisfied beyond the limits of the existing system.

Now the mass can only acquire and strengthen this will in the course of the day-to-day struggle against the existing social order—that is, within the limits of capitalist society.

On the one hand, we have the mass; on the other, its historic goal, located outside of existing society. On one hand, we have the day-to-day struggle; on the other, the social revolution. Such are the terms of the dialectical contradiction through which the socialist movement makes its way.

It follows that this movement can best advance by tacking betwixt and between the two dangers by which it is constantly being threatened. One is the loss of its mass character; the other, the abandonment of its goal. One is the danger of sinking back to the condition of a sect; the other, the danger of becoming a movement of bourgeois social reform.

That is why it is illusory, and contrary to historic experience, to hope to fix, once for always, the direction of the revolutionary socialist struggle with the aid of formal means, which are expected to secure the labor movement against all possibilities of opportunist digression.

Marxist theory offers us a reliable instrument en-

abling us to recognize and combat typical manifestations of opportunism. But the socialist movement is a mass movement. Its perils are not the
product of the insidious machinations of individuals and groups. They arise out of unavoidable social conditions. We cannot secure ourselves in advance against all possibilities of opportunist devia-
tion. Such dangers can be overcome only by the
movement itself—certainly with the aid of Marxist
theory, but only after the dangers in question have
taken tangible form in practice.

Looked at from this angle, opportunism appears
to be a product and an inevitable phase of the historic development of the labor movement.

The Russian Social Democracy arose a short while
ago. The political conditions under which the proletarian movement is developing in Russia are quite
abnormal. In that country, opportunism is to a
large extent a by-product of the groping and experi-
mentation of socialist activity seeking to advance
over a terrain that resembles no other in Europe.

In view of this, we find most astonishing the claim
that it is possible to avoid any possibility of opportunism in the Russian movement by writing down
certain words, instead of others, in the party constitution. *Such an attempt to exorcise opportunism
by means of a scrap of paper may turn out to be ex-
tremely harmful—not to opportunism but to the
socialist movement.*

Very
Import.

Stop the natural pulsation of a living organism,
and you weaken it, and you diminish its resistance
and combative spirit—in this instance, not only
against opportunism but also (and that is certainly
of great importance) against the existing social or-

der. The proposed means turn against the end they are supposed to serve.

In Lenin's overanxious desire to establish the guardianship of an omniscient and omnipotent Central Committee in order to protect so promising and vigorous a labor movement against any misstep, we recognize the symptoms of the same subjectivism that has already played more than one trick on socialist thinking in Russia.

It is amusing to note the strange somersaults that the respectable human "ego" has had to perform in recent Russian history. Knocked to the ground, almost reduced to dust, by Russian absolutism, the "ego" takes revenge by turning to revolutionary activity. In the shape of a committee of conspirators, in the name of a nonexistent Will of the People, it seats itself on a kind of throne and proclaims it is all-powerful. [The reference is to the conspiratorial circle which attacked tsarism from 1879 to 1883 by means of terrorist acts and finally assassinated Alexander II.—Translator.] But the "object" proves to be the stronger. The knout is triumphant, for tsarist might seems to be the "legitimate" expression of history.

In time we see appear on the scene an even more "legitimate" child of history—the Russian labor movement. For the first time, bases for the formation of a real "people's will" are laid in Russian soil.

But here is the "ego" of the Russian revolutionary again! Pirouetting on its head, it once more proclaims itself to be the all-powerful director of history—this time with the title of His Excellency the Central Committee of the Social Democratic Party of Russia.

The nimble acrobat fails to perceive that the only

"subject" which merits today the role of director is the collective "ego" of the working class. The working class demands the right to make its mistakes and learn in the dialectic of history.

Let us speak plainly. Historically, the errors committed by a truly revolutionary movement are infinitely more fruitful than the infallibility of the cleverest Central Committee.

SELECTED READINGS

Besides the two pamphlets here reissued the following works of Rosa Luxemburg are available in English translation:

The Crisis in the German Social Democracy, originally published under the pseudonym "Junius," and here erroneously attributed to Karl Liebknecht (New York, no date—probably 1918).

The Mass Strike, the Political Party and the Trade Union, translated by Patrick Lavin (Detroit, no date—probably 1919).

Reform or Revolution, translated by Integer (New York, 1937).

The Accumulation of Capital, translated by Agnes Schwarzchild (New Haven, 1951).

Rosa Luxemburg, Letters to Karl and Luise Kautsky, translated by Louis P. Lochner (New York, 1952).

The last named contains a brief biographical sketch of Rosa Luxemburg by Luise Kautsky. There is also a full-length biography by one who, in his zeal as an admirer both of Lenin and Luxemburg, does his best to blunt and obscure the differences they had with each other: *Rosa Luxemburg, Her Life and Works,* by Paul Froehlich (London, 1940).

Selected Ann Arbor Paperbacks
Works of enduring merit

For a complete list of Ann Arbor Paperback titles write:

THE UNIVERSITY OF MICHIGAN PRESS ANN ARBOR